Yes, Mrs. Williams

Books by

William Carlos Williams

A Personal Record

by William

of My Mother

Yes,
Mrs. Williams

Carlos Williams

MCDOWELL, OBOLENSKY / NEW YORK

TO HER GRANDCHILDREN

Yes, Mrs. Williams

Introduction

Determined women have governed my fate. Brought up on stories of my family, to whom I was devoted though I did not always approve of them, I made my way looking under every stone if need be to get on in the way I wanted to go.

My mother was half French, out of Martinique, the other half was a mixed breed, the Hohebs, Monsantos, I have already written too much about them. Her mother, Meline Hurrard or Hurrand, was of Basque stock. My father was English, typically English, as I learned to know him during my growing years. Obstinate but gentle in his nature, always a true gentleman, he never became a citizen of the United States though he made no objection to my remaining one after I had been born in the country.

My father, as a child of five, came to the States with my grandmother. He used to tell me, when I was very young, a wild story of going aground on Fire Island shoal when they had first crossed from England, of a bowsprit looming through the fog, and of the first few crowded hours at the Battery. When my grandmother remarried, to an itinerant photographer up in New York from St. Thomas for the purchase of supplies, she went with her son to that island where he was to grow up. Consequently, in the States where I was born, our earliest acquaintances were all English: the Hazels, the Lambs, the Dodds, and whoever it might be. Many of them the wives of sailing captains, the Forbes, Heitman, and Bushes with whom grandma had become intimate in St. Thomas and later in Puerto Plata when she was taken there by her husband following his trade. These made up the names of the first families I became acquainted with.

Years later, as a consequence, our house was always full of strangers, Casey Wright used to dig in our vegetable garden for the pupa of moths. I can still see them fitfully moving as he dug them up. There was Tinoco, the gentlemanly Mexican, a clerk in the office of Lanman & Kemp where my father was advertising manager at the time in charge of the presses.

It was an office in which Spanish was the language spoken among the staff. My father spoke Spanish quite as easily as he spoke English; he would never have been employed there if it had been otherwise. So that when I was a child Spanish was the language spoken in the household except by Mrs. Wellcome, my father's mother, who, when there was need of it, employed what was called *español de cocina,* pig Spanish, which was not pretty to hear.

So that as children my brother and I heard Spanish constantly spoken about us. A steady flow of West Indians, South Americans, and other speakers of the Spanish language came to visit us, to stay sometimes the entire winter if it so fitted their fancy or the necessity of the case. French we did not hear very much though we were conscious of it from the letters Mother occasionally received from Paris, a reminder of those fabulous friends she had once lived with on the Boulevard St. Germain just after the Franco-Prussian War in the later '70s when my mother had been an art student at the Académie des Beaux-Arts for three miraculous years. How else should I have heard of her teacher Carolous Durand, of J. J. Henner, and of all the parties her cousins Alice and Ludovic Monsanto, poor as church mice, saw that she was invited to.

I know now that Mother was not aware of the great names, Cézanne, Van Gogh, Gauguin, or anything of the rumors of the great exhibitions at the galleries of those years. She was no more than an obscure art student from Puerto Rico, slaving away at her trade which she loved with her whole passionate soul, living it, drinking it down with her every breath—the money gone, her mother as well as her father now dead, she was forced to return with her scanty laurels, a Grand Prix, a few gold medals to disappear into a trunk in my attic, a few charcoal sketches, a full length portrait of herself, unfinished, by that Ludovic, showing her ungainly hands.

From Paris she returned to these meager islands. She married at the home of one of those same Monsantos and pretty soon had two boys on her hands. I call it her vicarious atonement. Her heart was broken. No doubt she had been much of a spoiled brat, but there were ample precedents for her depressed mood which sometimes overcame her, and she was tough and willing—and full of fire when she was called upon to show it.

All my life, kid-like, I had been interested in my father's head, its size. He wore a 7½ hat. I frequently tried it on, its shape and general attitude facing the world. Who was he? He was too young when he quit England to remember anything and his own mother was adamant in her refusal to disclose what I most wanted to know. There is one daguerreotype showing a brilliant and self-confident smile on that small face, a picture showing a London photographer's label. That is all. He was an intelligent and handsome child.

There was Godwin, Father's half brother, who died in early manhood. He was fat and loved to dance, a wonderful companion for my brother and me during my early boyhood when we were living at the Baggellen house in East Rutherford. All sorts of things fascinating to a child there. For it was a huge building with a porch that ran entirely around it and with a cupola on top from which, through a telescope, I once looked at the moon. It was a run-down farm which there was no one to take care of on the outskirts of town. We lived there on one of the frequent and prolonged periods when my father was in Central or South America. A whole book could be written about that.

But the point of this is the name Godwin. My grandmother, born in Kent, had been left an orphan in Chichester and was picked up by a well-to-do London family by the name of Godwin. This is the name that grandmother had given her youngest child. Now the Godwins were a well-known family in London. William Godwin's wife was Mary Wollstonecraft, the intimate of Percy Bysshe Shelley, and the whole lot of them supporters of the principle of free love. God knows of the intimacies of my grandmother and the set that surrounded her in those years; we have only evidence of it in her devotion to the name of Godwin which she gave her child.

Though this book is mainly about my mother, and should be so, it must dwell somewhat for its character on the man she lived with most of her life, my father. He, as far as anyone could, influenced her as he took care of her in the years before he died. He confided to me just before the end that she was a strange creature and cautioned me that I would have my trouble with her. But this is merely an excuse for speaking of him here.

My father was a great storyteller. His accounts of his travels muleback over Costa Rica, the eating of the *pâtés* of black ants when caught short for a meal far out in the mountains held me rapt. His story of Bluebeard's castle, from his own childhood in St. Thomas, he made thoroughly familiar to me, as well as the story of the great earthquake and tidal wave that followed it in the early seventies: how the sea retreated, leaving the ships that were in the harbor at the time stranded on their beams' end. They thought the whole island from moment to moment was going to disappear under the water.

Be his antecedents what they may, my father always took pride in himself as a gentleman. He was curiously mild. I don't think I ever saw him really angry until once when he attempted to force me to eat a tomato, which I detested— then he attempted to jam the fruit down my throat, but he never did that again.

He loved to read before anything else, even before working in his garden. He invariably spoke with a distinguished choice of his words. It sometimes exasperated me. One of the books on his library shelf was Archbishop Trench on words. He was a liberal and somewhat of a socialist. He, along with my mother, was one of the founders of the Unitarian Society of Rutherford. I attended its Sunday school from the first when it was no more than a room over a store on Park Avenue. As boys my brother and I knew all the New Englanders who made up the majority of the congregation, including E. J. Luce, the crusty organist, a prominent lawyer of the town who gave me my first look at the *Symposium.*

As soon as I became conscious of a library in the house, occupying a few shelves in "the back parlor." I was introduced to Charles Darwin's *The Descent of Man* and *The Origin of Species,* which I read avidly and could never forget. Among my random reading there was the philosophy of Herbert Spencer, but his habit of dictating to an amanuensis while in the act of rowing a boat impressed me more than did his text. I remember seeing and reading there at least the beginning of *The Canterbury Tales,* though I did not read the story of *Troilus and Cressida* till much later. But my real love was for Palgrave's *Golden Treasury of English Verse* leading to the *Endymion* . . . but of that more later.

My father's greatest love was for Shakespeare which he read extremely well and without affectation. I heard all the principal plays with few exceptions during the long winter evenings when he would read to the family, for I must say that he did not read particularly to me, but to Mother as much as anyone else.

In the same way he read the dialect poems of Paul Laurence Dunbar. I enjoyed them at the time quite as much as the others. For we were not an especially literary family, but loved to read anything, anything that came along. The copy of Dante's *Inferno,* with full-page engravings by Gustave Doré was left undisturbed. It was known to me chiefly because of the magnificent nude figures of damned and beautiful ladies of antiquity who scared me, but I came back time after time to them, sneaking a look, when I thought that no one was looking.

I heard read, to my mother, of course, in the night when I was presumed to be asleep, whatever forbidden novels came to my parents attention and that they cared to play with. I remember hearing, as much as I could stay awake for, DuMaurier's *Trilby*, with the particular delight of a child taking part in something that has been forbidden. My father was not one to keep anything from me if he thought I could understand it. His first job when he sought employment at St. Thomas was as a rum taster, at which he is reputed to have worked successfully for several years. He was never a drinker, but always had liquor in the house. As kids we were asked not to drink it until we had reached the age of twenty-one—the same with tobacco. Leave it alone for the present. We did what Pop asked us to, for the most part. But at Christmas we were given a sip of gin fizz which had been prepared at the table. We always had a "booze closet" unlocked in the dining room. I can remember my father wielding the swizzle stick, twirling it between his fingers, and the delight he took in the antics of Mrs. D. when she had no more than her first drink.

Pop learned to play the flute when he was a young man in St. Thomas, at about the same time as his half brother Irving, who remained always better at it than he. There was a story about him at that time, getting hold of a piano, determined to learn to play it. It was just when he must have been courting Mother, fresh from Paris with her romantic nature! Poor Pop. His best friend was Carlos Hoheb, Dr. Carlos Hoheb, Elena's brother, an accomplished musician.

Carlos, who could have made a name for himself in New York, as a surgeon or an orchestra conductor—a man I missed knowing to my infinite loss by the chances of a lifetime—was consulted by his sister on a general subject: the desirability of this young man as sister's suitor.

Williams is a fine young man. I like him very much. *Pero no es musicante*—he is no musician.

Every once in a while my father and his brother would get out their flutes and with my mother's assistance at the piano put on a little concert of a Sunday evening, private of course. My uncle was indulgent, as he well needed to be, living in our house. He never did very much to support himself except during the years he was in Johannesburg, South Africa, when he sent my father the triangular postage stamps which rapidly became rare and were used to piece out the cost of our education.

When Georgie, our colored girl, who could peg a stone left-handed over the top of the chestnut tree next door, which neither of us boys could do, when this Georgie climbed over the top of the grape arbor back of us to get into her room at two A.M. Pop knew about it, as he always did. Next morning at breakfast table with sleepy-eyed Georgie stumbling over serving him, he let her have it. That word out of my father's mouth surprised me; it hurt, but it was meant to—straight from the West Indies. It had surprised *him*.

Suddenly, in the middle of winter, January, 1897, father, returning home from his job in New York, announced to us we were to quit school. He had arranged passage for us on the French liner, *La Touraine;* all of us were going abroad to France! To Switzerland where my brother and (what I am attempting is a portrait of my father and mother in the light of what they did for me) I were to be put in a school. It fulfilled my mother's most cherished dream, to return to France, of which her mind had never lost one moment of its loyalty day or night for going on twenty years.

I was only thirteen years old. When the boat landed the first thing I heard from the country I was about to visit for the first time, repeated over and over in a childish girl's voice, was:

> Vois la d'jolis violettes!
> Vois la d'jolis violettes!
> Vois la d'jolis violettes!

. . . uttered by a flower vender holding up a bunch of the sweet–scented blossoms which she had herself gathered for me to buy. They were the first words in the French language I heard.

This violent change in my fortunes altered the whole perspective of my life. We remained, my brother and I, for a year and a half in Switzerland during which we encountered a new language, first at the Château de Lancy and later in Paris where we attended, briefly, the Lycée Condorcet, unfortunately not long enough to do us much good.

A Swiss springtime, when I was still a young boy, made

a deep impression on me, with my stealing of birds' eggs and the knocking of my head against Leon Pont's when I was caught by Madam Haccius, and grapes from over the school wall.

I had an experience with a bearded and monocled old man when, in the following months, I was being taken for a *tour du lac* by my mother, but I was not ready for it and it made little impression.

In Paris we went to live with my cousin Alice and her husband, a lawyer out of a job, at 42 rue la Bruyère, in a poorer section of the city. M. Trufley was lame from a wound received *dans la guerre* and lived on a pension, which my cousin always sought to waylay before M. Trufley could get his hands on it to spend on his absinthe which he lived by. He was a former employee of the de Lesseps Company of Panama where he had met his wife. He came of a family which had a small estate in Normandy, now gone into thin air, of which he occasionally spoke with a wry smile.

But M. Trufley with his sparse goatee was a great guy to me. Escaping his wife under guise of taking his young cousins to see the sights of Paris he would be sipping his absinthe while we were drinking our *sirop de groseille*. We saw Paris from the catacombs to the museums. We went to the Folies Bergère, on my mother's money I suspect, even one night to Le Néant and heard them sing:

> *Tous les clients*
> *sont des cochons*
> *Le follis don dell*
> *le follis do don*

Trufley was known all over the city and though he had no money was welcomed everywhere. His limping up the Boulevard des Italiens during a downpour, his naked cane raised protectively above his head, was to me the eternal Frenchman in his better moments as we sometimes pictured him.

I stared into the windows of the exhibitors of paintings, before which I passed on my way about the street to and from my fencing lessons. We were followed by some young man who had been attracted by our youth and obvious strangeness to the city. I went on my own, through the Boulevard ankle-deep in confetti, witnessing during the *Carnaval* some of the more exciting sights that surrounded me, heard the screams of the girls pressed against the walls by the young men following them right and left. Ignorant of the world I was no more than a boy lost in an adult world, tempted on every side, like how many others. Mother could do nothing about it—but she was there. I tried my best, but I knew that I was lying to her every moment of the day. It was more than I could control.

When with my brother I returned from France, I was sent as usual to the best school that could be found in the region, the Horace Mann High School in New York City. Maybe it was worth it.

In my later teens my father and brother and I used to go on long walks during our summer vacations. This must have been in the early years of the century before the appearance of the automobile on the roads spoiled everything. One summer, particularly, we set out just above Paterson late in the afternoon, heading for Sloatsburg.

We tried one back door for a night's lodging and were told to keep going and finally landed in an inn on the main road which cannot have been much frequented—it was too late in the century for much carriage trade there. The beds however were clean. Early next morning we had our eggs and bacon and coffee and that day did our twenty-three or more miles, crossing the Hudson by ferry to hole up at Fishkill across the river from Newburgh.

That was a very romantic interlude in which I got to know my father better than I had ever known him previously. "Put foot!" said he to us one morning when we were starting the day's walk, pure St. Thomas English, I've kept it in mind ever since. Curving back of Beacon Mountain we got as far that day as Washington, Connecticut, thirty-two miles. Not bad for a man his age. I remember how we used to take the road, at times fifty or sixty feet apart, not talking together for half an hour, perhaps longer. We enjoyed it. We must have been an uncommunicative tribe though we could talk, plenty, when we were spurred to it.

The whole comedy was to end at this stage of my progress in the hilarious farce of our good intentions, as a family, myself the elder son taking the lead. There was no family in the country, in the world, that meant better than we did. Our mother was an angel. When, after my internship at the French Hospital, I accepted a further year's residency at the Nursery and Childs on my way to becoming an accredited New York specialist, the family was elated.

First, the bare facts of the controversy: Wide-eyed, though not completely innocent, I entered my new duties.

Nothing could have appeared more acceptable to the young physician than this turn of his fortunes. A residency at the Nursery and Childs—in "Hell's Kitchen" by the way, though he was not aware of it at the time—was just what he wanted, a place where, as Fatty the head nurse would say, there were babies fresh every hour, one hundred percent illegitimate. After the first six months as a junior, I was in charge. At once all hell broke out. It was a scream.

It was the first of the new month. The tormented secretary of the Board of Governors unobtrusively placed a paper on my desk that required my signature. It was the report to Albany of the roster of children registered in the hospital files. Oh sweet and innocent parents who have taught me the way to go! I asked to see the records. I was ignored. Consequently I would not sign. But it was a state report and no one could take the place of the Resident Physician.

Things began to happen. The merriment broke out and increased momentarily. No one could do what I had determined not to do. *Cherchez la femme!* It went all the way from the chief of the medical staff among the attending physicians at the hospital, a man at the top of his profession in the city to whom I was myself beholden for my own appointment on the staff, to the whole body of physicians who were involved. I began to feel at that time the drive of my fate, that there was something in the wind more powerful than I knew. Adamant, I would not be moved until—I had a lucky break. It came in the form of a hell of a sore throat.

One of my pals on the nursing staff, I always had 'em,

came to me in my sick room, all out of breath. She had just seen the President of the Board of Governors, standing before his secretary, a middle-aged woman on her knees before him . . . the Satyrs, with obscene gestures, contorted themselves across the scene screaming with laughter in which we joined them. It was a scandalous story. It had come too late. I had already written a letter resigning my post at the hospital. My career as a New York physician was cut short.

Returning home, my parents received me as usual, understandingly. My brother Ed had been a brilliant student of architecture at Boston Tech. We have always been a closely knit family, relying on each other when the chips were down. Just at the moment the American Prix de Rome competition for 1908 was about to be decided. Ed was in the final brackets of the competition. Pop said, I can't afford to send you both abroad, but if Ed wins I'll send you to Germany—where I elected to go, much to Ezra Pound's disgust, for a year.

I had just proposed to Flossie. Everything was going with a rush. Ed clinched it by winning the Prix de Rome. Flossie, only ninteen at the time and somewhat uncertain, consented to be married on my return from abroad. I plunged at once into a play I was in the act of writing, all thought of medicine for the moment forgotten or almost.

I was poised on the brink of what my life was to bring, on the verge of what a year in Germany, at work in the classrooms and clinics of Leipzig, Auerbach's Keller, the plays of Ibsen, the opera, Strauss's *Elektra*, etc. was to bring; a week in London with Pound at 10 Church Walk, the English countryside in April with the violets in full bloom, and most of all over Spain and Italy with my brother. Ah!

When my mother had got through with her painting, we had left her half-squeezed-out tubes in our attic, with their memory of d'Archambeau and Ludovic, to play with for years. She couldn't sing as she got older, and in fact, her attempts to do so set our teeth on edge. We hated it. But she still had her piano. It was a comfort to her as she got older, a reminder of the days when she could still sing her arias from *La Traviata* and her teacher would encourage her, *Allez, allez! ma petite!*

Living in the suburbs as we did, our gang, during the past twenty or thirty years, to relieve the occasional monotony of our lives, formed a group which we called the Polytopic Club. At one time I was elected president of the entertainment committee. I developed the curious idea to have a reading of poems from the masters, but the feature of this reading, this dramatic reading, was to be that it would be in the original language in every case. We had some unexploited talent in the club, as will be seen, my mother among them, more or less as a hanger-on. She loved to listen, but seldom took part in the programs.

This time we had the Superintendent of schools read a passage from the *Odyssey,* from the Greek original. We listened attentively and heard, in a measured voice, a passage that sounded like Calvin Coolidge at his most inspired. I did my best to keep my face under control.

My brother, who knew his *vero toscano* and could deliver it with distinction, gave a passage from Dante's *Inferno,* the passage where Ulysses, his ship foundered, saw it disappear from mortal sight under the sea. Ed did it extremely well. I have never forgotten it. We had readings from Shakespeare, from Virgil, from Lope de Vega, from Faust and Bobby Burns from a Scotsman among the club members.

Then, the meeting at our house, it came my mother's turn to do her bit. She was almost blind with cataracts, but when I called on her, the room anticipating what was to take place, was intently listening. We could have heard ourselves breathe. Taking her time she delivered, in French, a speech from Corneille ending in the famous curse. *Rome enfin que je hais!* which left us speechless. All her contempt and even hatred that we had earned in this benighted country through the years was contained in that anathema. She finished and from the depth of her soul it came out, but good. She sat back, her cheeks were aflame, her audience was spellbound.

Now I have to report a curious phenomenon. Out of the blue about seventy years ago, at the supper table, something happened to Mother. It was a seizure of some sort, but she did not lose consciousness, her alertness rather was quickened, concentrated, brought to a point—or so it seemed. I myself was too young the first time to make any proper estimate of it. I got to hate the things as they recurred from time to time in the following years. They scared me.

Ed and I were just children, but we realized at once the seriousness of the stituation. We cooperated with Father when he told us what to do. She indicated that she wanted us, her children, to come on either side of her, which we did. She placed her hands on our heads.

So these are the children. How they have grown.

Then she caressed us, patted our heads and kissed us. And who is this? said Pop.

Don't you know me? answered my mother. Lou Payne.

And with that the occasion ended, Mother relaxed and went on with her supper. The sequel is interesting. For Father at once sent a telegram to Jessie, Lou's husband, living with his wife in Los Angeles. Has anything happened to Lou?

For two weeks no reply came, then there was an answer apologizing for the delay: When I received your wire Lou was on the operating table. We thought she had died. But under artificial respiration she started to breathe again. When I had your telegram I couldn't think of anything else but her care.

All during her life such incidents recurred at the most inopportune times, in church or funerals wherever she was emotionally roused, but never as startlingly as this time.

These seizures finally changed to an occupation with dreams. She had her favorites about whom to dream. This was when she was almost blind, when in my opinion it was a compensation for her failing vision. In her dreams she could see perfectly well. Mr. Luce, now many years dead, often stood beside her, occupied with whatever he had to do. She loved to have him about.

Once she described him with the minutest accuracy with a piece of knitting in his hands. She was fully aware of the humor of the situation, Luce, a man, at a woman's occupation! She was fascinated. To hear her tell it, she watched him with the greatest admiration, the minute stitches hour after hour. Beautiful! She didn't dare disturb him or he might stop. What a wonderful experience. But New Englanders are that way sometimes, they make wonderful apple pies and fine needlework when put to it. Mr. Luce was a typical New Englander whom she had the deepest affection for.

So she retreated to her dreams.

She died with a tranquil smile on her face, just went to sleep from pneumonia. What dream she was following at the moment of course we will never know. The truth and its pursuit was always at the front of my mother's mind. It was a long time before I came to realize how her romantic ideas had deceived her and me in the modern world which we in our turn had to push behind us to come up fighting or smiling, if we could make it, or just to find some sunny spot where we could stretch our bones, even if we had a broken hip like Mother, and not complain. She did pretty well, as Pop did before her. With her, Ai! Ai! Ai! which I can still hear in the night, as much as to say, give me a drink—of water! that's all she would ever touch to relieve her of her pain except, on rare occasions, a swallow of whisky in the night to put her to sleep again: it meant nothing more to her.

When Mother and I began to translate *The Dog and the Fever,* I knew no more of Quevedo than the bawdy reports reputed to him which had come down the two hundred years after his death even to Mayagüez and so on to me. That's a rather long life for casual reports, since the time of Shakespeare; many a man would be happy with far less fame. I'm sure Mother knew no more than I of the man, though it was his name which attracted us to the book which we finally took up and began to work on. It was something Ezra Pound had left in the house during one of his passages; I always wanted to know what the man meant by such a title, *The Dog and the Fever.* So we began to translate, and it was tough going.

The last few pages of the book in particular were impossible for us and, as I found, for others better qualified than we to dig out a meaning from that purposed jumble. Quevedo had made it a jumble or an apparent jumble in order to hide the facts he didn't dare tell outright, and refused at the same time to let lie. He just couldn't keep quiet.

The last few pages are written in what I am told was the slang of the day, that is of the early seventeenth century about the court in Madrid, the language of the vulgar which Quevedo took great delight in flinging in the teeth of the refined and corrupt taste of his day. He was like that. His youth was like that of Góngora, especially, having been spent among all classes from top to bottom of Spanish society. He knew the whole gamut of his world, and used his knowledge against cads and numskulls in or out of power.

In Salamanca, at college, he got his face scarred by swordplay in duels, and finally ended by killing an opponent, while his savage wit made him feared on all sides. And famous. His scholarship was no less renowned: in Hebrew, Greek, Latin and several of the modern languages of his time. Like Byron, he was born an aristocrat, poor and lame—though in *both* feet—and walked all his life with a shuffle. But unlike Byron, he was stocky and powerful in his shoulders, like a bull, and half-blind, like a bull also, and wore large, heavy glasses—in 1590!

When the excitement caused by the fatality resulting from his collegiate dueling had subsided, and Quevedo was able to return to the normal life of Madrid, he continued his studies and was shortly invited to join himself with his patron, the Duke of Mendoza, with whom he left shortly for Sicily and grew to know the writers of that time who were beginning to revive the culture of the Renaissance in Rome and elsewhere.

Here Quevedo performed many distinguished services in a political and diplomatic capacity, but returning to Spain after several years was falsely accused of slanders of which he was not, as it happened, the originator. He was arrested, tried, and condemned to prison. His lands were confiscated and it looked as though he had come to the end of his rope. Illness overtook him and he prepared to die. He never perhaps recovered his health after this trial —which embittered him more than anything.

So much for Quevedo. I might have gone on writing a scholarly thesis upon his name or upon the occasion of his composition of *The Dog and the Fever,* what he meant by such a title in relation to the times in which he wrote. But what do I know of those times? Nothing. I am not a student of Spanish history, and what I should write would be at best secondhand—as I found out once, when I wrote of the poet Lorca, and no one was interested.

But what I can write about is the woman who did, in effect, most of the translation: my mother. So that for the balance of this book, counting on her natural sympathy for Quevedo to bridge the gap, I shall speak from now on about my mother, as if my mother were still living.

Now, past eighty, the way she talks is this: When Puerto Rico belonged to the Spanish and the regiments would come—young officers from Andalusia and Castilla—they would take their capes and throw them before the feet of the girls they admired. *Dichosa es la madre que te pario!* they would say. Happy is the mother who bore you! And they would throw flowers . . . *Echando flores!* Such flowers! Such flowers!

All that is changed now I suppose.

All sorts of things like that would come out of her from time to time. I got into the habit of writing them down —on the back of an envelope, on any piece of scrap paper I could lay my hands on quickly—so as to preserve the flavor and the accurate detail.

Often, though her eyes have been failing in recent years, she would detect me and ask what I was doing. I just want to remember some of these things, Mother—to tell the boys sometime—and for their own sakes. It's interesting.

Don't you write about me, she would say—but I confess that I paid little attention to her.

She is still full of violent gestures, throwing things out of her hands when she is through with them, not watching where they fall—then looking for them afterward, perhaps. Not that she isn't orderly. Quite the contrary. As she began to grow toward blindness she began to arrange her possessions, to the last spool of thread in her table drawer, so that she could put her hand on them later.

She is about to pass out of the world; I want to hold her back a moment for her to be seen because—in many ways I think she is so lovely, for herself, that it would be a pity if she were lost without something of her—something impressed with her mind and her spirit—herself—remaining to perpetuate her—for our profit.

When this is written she is in her eighty-third year—unless I am greatly mistaken—a small woman with straggling white hair, clumsy hands, lame, extremely deaf and only recently recovered from the removal of cataracts from both eyes—waiting to see if, with time, she will be able to read again. For all her impatience of disposition—and she would never have broken her hip if she had listened to me—she has been very patient during these last difficult years.

She had bought a new fur coat and was going to wear it to the Reading Club one day. That was a Monday. The day before, Sunday, she had been to church without rubbers—she is still extremely vain of her small feet. There were patches of thin ice on the pavements and Mr. Tufts had forbidden her to walk home. She would have paid no attention to him, but he, being a New Englander, was even more positive than she and practically forced her into his car.

She was furious and when I opened the door for her she said several uncomplimentary things about him to me under her breath. He merely smiled at me and I nodded.

The next day, though she had the warning clearly in mind, because of it perhaps, to show her indifference, she went to the Club, along the icy roadway—without rubbers —and in spite of the fact that I had advised her to take a taxi. She fell. She fell in the middle of the roadway and couldn't get up. She sustained an intracapsular fracture of the left hip.

In spite of excellent treatment she has never been able to walk again.

As the years went by I found myself under the necessity of entertaining her as best I could while she sat in her room year in and year out—though this enforced rest and idleness without question have made it possible for her to go on living in excellent general health to this date. It is a point the old should take to heart.

Once we translated a French novel together. Then, finally, I hit on the scheme I wanted. Casting about for something to translate, the fit object offered itself in the form of an old book. I got the book from Ezra Pound, it was a purely accidental occurrence; he never as far as I remember spoke to me of the book thereafter. He was not interested in Spanish literature so much as in Italian and the literature of Provence. I don't think he spoke Spanish; certainly I never heard him speak it to my mother, though she knew him well.

There it is. Let that be the scaffolding. I'll speak of all these things as if she told them to me while we were translating—only the pretext: the real story is how all the complexities finally came to play one tune, today—to me—what I find good in my own life. She has lived through—and stands an example of that.

I enjoyed this contact with her and then, I think, conceived the idea of gathering her sayings which interested and amused me.

For she speaks three languages with considerable ease—English the least perfectly, but for that very reason what she says in English—with Spanish and French words and sayings intermixed—fascinated me the more. I began to copy down her phrases. I collected all kinds of notes.

Lame from the accident to her hip, confined to her room, this made it easier for me to talk to her—but harder to amuse her. We had difficult times.

From this grew the idea of the biography, though not without certain hazards putting themselves in the way, hazards which had to be vaulted. She would catch sight of me out of the corner of her eye putting down something she had just said on the back of an envelope.

What are you writing there, she would say accusingly.

Oh, just something I want to remember.

Are you writing down what I say, because if you are . . .

Well, Mother, after all. I like to remember those proverbs

you tell me. I think they are worth preserving. She wasn't fooled.

I don't want you to write my biography, she said. My life is too mixed up.

So much the more reason, my dear, I answered her. For here you are.

Very unhappy . . .

Very happily, my mother! I made a bow. She smiled. Why even Captain Stousland, I went on, who looks the picture of Ibsen and is in fact his second cousin, admired you.

I don't remember him.

Just this morning, in the post office, he asked after you again. He has never forgotten how you recited that speech from *Phèdre* that night . . . *Rome enfin que je hais!* Do you remember?

Yes, I remember.

It is in complexities that appear finally as one person that the good of a life shows itself—bringing all together to return the world to simplicity again: this is her life. An interesting life because, I believe, in essence it is a good life as she has been a good woman—not good in a sense of being morally virtuous—because perhaps it was that too—but good in the sense of being a valuable thing to me, when I think about it, a thing of value—like a good picture: a sharp differentiation of good from evil —something to look at and to know with satisfaction, some- thing alive—that has partaken of many things, welcom- ing them indiscriminately if they seemed to have a value —a color—a sound to add still more to the intelligent, the colorful, the whole grasp of feeling and knowledge in the world.

So, looking for something else to translate before the cataracts would make it impossible for her to see anything for a while, I hit upon the book, which gave me the clue to how my composition should be formed. A story turning about a story. I shall make it seem as if she told me her life while we were working over the translation, then as if we looked up from that work, speak as if she were telling me about herself.

Our family is among those who came to America from Europe through the West Indies—so that in the United States—since they still owned slaves in Puerto Rico—I feel more southern than the southerners, and by virtue of my father, who was born in England, as northern as if I had come from Maine.

Here is something Mother herself wrote one day—precisely as she wrote it:

Dear Sonny: Sitting in my room as usual, the thought came to my mind that some time ago you came to my room and you said something about knowing your ancestors, perhaps you would like some details. I am the last of the old stock and I don't know much, I only have (Ed has it) an interesting daguerreotype of my maternal grandfather, he was a native of France, pure Frenchman, an "armateur" or privateer (equipment of a ship or fleet) and traveled much; he married a Martinican girl and had three daughters, Colette, Caroline, Meline the younger was my mother. My father was from Holland extraction, he was a merchant associated with two Germans in Mayagüez, Puerto Rico, they received cargos from Europe of rice, flour and I don't know what. I was only eight years old when I lost my father, I didn't know much; a fierce dog was put at night

to guard the cargo newly arrived, the name of the dog was
Moro. One night he came home like a demon dragging his long
chain. It had rained much and the earth was mud, he went to
my father's room howl and howl went all over, the house was
in mourning the master was gone. Wasn't that strange?

If I love Spain so much it is because I had friends so dear
to me and I never will forget them. I lived with them. Now,
the present Spain with the civil war so unnecessary and so
stupid makes me feel quite sad.

I have to stop, writing is very hard for me now, but I wanted
to have a little chat with you.

Nana

I put down here what is to follow because the book will
be that way—to show how the book is likely to be. I find
that it belongs here. An interval.

A friend had sent a gardenia up to her on New Year's
Day—strong-scented tropical flowers always appeal to her
—and she had me put it in a narrow vial. I came up later
to take her down to lunch and found her standing, the
flower in a different vase from the one I had chosen, clutch-
ing the back of a chair with one hand, in the other a
single red rose, with a pair of scissors dangling from one
finger. Maddening. She had been fixing things the way
she wanted them. There's always some sort of petty feud
going on between us.

Why didn't you let me do that? You might fall.

If you leave it in the water it will take roots, she said
turning toward the gardenia. Then you can plant it (I
saw her vision growing into a small bush), and it will
grow.

Really? Be careful you don't fall.

Yes. You must leave it there, because the same deposit of the water helps to create roots, she said. I put it there to leave for a month, perhaps more than a month. Then you can see the roots coming down.

A spoiled child!

There would be less point to this book were it not that her father was, as many had been before him, a patient man by the name of Job. Though the precise truth of the matter is not known, the reason being that he was the only child of a widowed mother who married again during his infancy; he grew up Enriquez, to assume his own name only in later life. Like the Job from whom his name was taken, he was a tirelessly patient and gentle man—not to say tragically aware of his fate at all times and a great lover of music.

Old Mrs. Wingate, Mother said, was the one who told me about my father. She said he was a great dancer in St. Thomas. That is where she knew him. All the girls wanted to dance with him.

In the West Indies, in Martinique, St. Thomas, Puerto Rico, Santo Domingo, in those days, the races of the world mingled and intermarried—imparting their traits one to another and forgetting the orthodoxy of their ancient and medieval views. It was a good thing. It is in the best spirit of the New World.

That it is good and that my mother is good by virtue of these things that she had taught me, I live largely to exemplify as best I may. If I speak of the good, not a single word of truth is presumed here—nothing but the words I know and set down for what they may be worth:

it is from being myself sure that if they are worth anything it will be in how closely they are able to approach all that which she, in herself, was and lived.

And if the world will not have it—if the world will not have her—then I will turn the world to my way, so that it cannot escape. It must take her as she is, good. It cannot do anything else—unless it is itself evil.

A life, a tough life, for she is still alive! and goes on living the same in spite of difficulties—particularly timely today. As to her toughness: If she hadn't been tough—in spite of her thin skin (nervousness, timidity, shyness)—she wouldn't have survived nor should I have been here to tell it. Good, then.

When she went to pay that long delayed call on Mrs. Cobham in Weehawken—some twenty years ago—it was one of the hottest days of the summer. She got lost among the strange streets, and with her feet burning went up to a cop to get her bearings. She had the house number, improperly written, on a slip of paper in her handbag which she always carried—to have something to keep her handkerchief in.

He looked at the piece of paper, looked at her, asked her if she was walking—which, obviously, she was—then, seeing she was an old lady, directed her to the street and number she wanted, and added the advice to take it easy, it was a very hot day.

Once more, arriving at the same wrong house she had found the first time, she went wandering about the blazing streets confused for another hour—without lunch, not knowing where she was or, properly, where she was going, till she came to the same cop standing on the same corner on which she had found him the first time.

When she came up he looked at her in amazement. Didn't you find it? he said.

No, said my mother.

And you've been walking these streets again all this time?

Yes, said she.

Well, you're tough, was his rejoinder. It was one of her favorite stories for many years. She would laugh hard every time she thought of it. Well, you're tough, he said standing there in the shade under an awning; she would repeat it over and over.

No way to speak of her other than by first setting up a sign, as in a dream, to the overwhelming beauty of the world and its overwhelming, such as the destruction of St. Pierre by the explosion of Mt. Pelée in 1902. Not that St. Pierre was so particularly beautiful—though such towns have their voluptuous plenty in spite of a certain heterogeneity of moral background. In any case all mark of one branch of her family seems to have been obliterated by that catastrophe, the Hurrards. They had a business there manufacturing a brand of liqueurs, so I have been told.

A sketch of her life—in its exterior details—before dipping into the proofs—She was born in Mayagüez, Puerto Rico, in 1855 or thereabouts—and lived there, in Mayagüez, through an early era of moderate prosperity while her father was alive, and considerable want after his death which took place in her eighth year. There were her mother, her brother, and herself, very close, three against fate.

When Carlos returned to the West Indies from Paris to practice medicine he soon saw to it that his sister was sent there after him to study—painting!—to sing—to find a way to earn her living.

Where do you want to go, he asked her, to the United States or to France?

To France! to FRANCE! to *FRANCE!* she cried!

The money failed—and there were other things. She returned to Puerto Rico (or was it Santo Domingo where her brother had gone by that time?)—her preparations for a career unfinished, heartbroken in her late twenties, to go to New York to marry, to come to New Jersey, to Rutherford! to live, to have children and to—exhale her fragrance —or lack of it—into the surrounding air.

If I can catch enough of it to make it seem—then it will have been proved to be! And one will have partaken of it, lived by it. Lived.

So grown old—in vain, a woman creates a son and dies in her own mind. That is the end. She is dead, she says. But that vigor for living, clinging desperately to the small threads of a reality which she thought to have left in Paris—the battle is against her. How continue to love in the face of defeat? *Why am I alive? No one can realize what I have desired. I succeeded in nothing, I have kept nothing, I am nothing.*

That is the defeated romantic. It is not by any means a true picture. Despondency, discouragement, despair were violent periodic factors in her life. Under it lies the true life, undefeated if embittered, hard as nails, little loving, easily mistaken for animal selfishness. Unexcavated from her own consciousness, the good that is in her—crying for release, release from herself, a most difficult animal. I never knew her to succumb long to her most profound depressions, but would see her come up again finally stronger than ever—despising only those who had been taken in before.

Witness her courage—difficulties quiet her, she is not led astray by false feeling. She remains unbroken.

If in a son one could live again! But it is impossible. And if you make it a work of the imagination, she might have said, it won't be me.

I'll fool you, old girl. I won't make it a work of the imagination. I'll make it you.

No. I died.

Why go on living then? Why eat like a pig and belch like one afterward. No, you didn't die. Now you . . . I don't care who you are unless you are what is imaginable and you are that. Don't think I don't know what old age does. You are nothing that you wanted to be, true enough, what *you* wanted to be. But something is alive that maybe you did not want to be. Something is there for all that. You have vanity enough, for an old woman, God knows!

Blind?

Any day now, I replied.

Not on your life. When the hairdresser cut her hair that way she was furious. She could see. Don't you fool yourself. Vanity! I said, another time. She sure has got it.

Good for her. I'm glad she's vain. One must be vain. She's right. I'm glad she's got it.

She's right if what lives is good, if it is valuable. If it has not been lost, degraded.

All the races of the earth mingled in the West Indies.
There were the Luchetties, the Gordons, the Wingwoods,
the Bryans, the Monsantos, the Kruegers, the Hurrards,
the Hazels—Jimmy Hazel, who owned the island in St.
Thomas Harbor and still owns it unless one of the big
oil companies has done him out of it by this time—the
Toledos, the Wrights—Casey Wright! who used to come
out to dig up chrysalises in our vegetable garden years
ago. It was not only a fact, it was at its best a revolution!
a revolution of sentiment and, through that, of the intelligence. Sentiment was the instigator. Patti, Gottschalk,
whoever it might be, came there to understanding and
liberation—while it lasted!—before the weight fell.

While it lasted—too lovely to last long—it threw its
light not far enough over the world, but there was light
there and in this light she grew up—tolerance, the break-
down of old rigidities. It was precisely this that the West
Indian tradition tended to break down—traditions they
had left behind, simply didn't know any more. This was its
good.

Evil opposed it. The line is sharply drawn as it is in the
character of my mother. Nothing infuriates her like in-
justice—she suffered for it.

Difficult to show, but I'll try. As she once said: *Dicen los
Españoles que con paciencia se gano el cielo.* Not missing
the cynical touch I seek nothing else.

At the beginning of 1936, before she had broken her leg
for the second time, what with her deafness and cataracts
it was becoming difficult to find or to make conversation
by which to divert her. There is an incentive arising from

the weak and the defenseless that drives us devilishly to want to insult and even to kill them. It is bestial in a man to want to slaughter his old mother—so that he had better find an alternative.

It took the form of an old book that had been lying about the house unread for many years. I had held it in my hands many times without ever having had the courage to dip into it, knowing it to be an early seventeenth-century Spanish text printed in a very wobbly looking face—a *novella.*

She has frequently in her life referred to Quevedo, telling one or another of the salty stories connected with his name, showing that she enjoyed them exceedingly well. Were it not for these stories she has told me, the old book would not have attracted me and nothing more would have come of it—even the idea of the biography would not have taken form beyond the vague idea I had of it. So that, by this, *El Perro y la Calentura* belongs here—and belongs to her.

It grew to be a device, as I thought more and more of my plan, quite as much to draw the story out of her as to string it together. But more than anything else it was to entertain her, and so belongs in the account. Like her it is old, though far older than she. It is an octavo of very much worn brown leather, with the title in crooked gilt letters, all but completely obliterated. The print is large, old fashioned, and irregularly spaced, and the punctuation is to say the least individual.

The various owners of the book since 1700 have scribbled their names and a few faded notes among the fly leaves at the front and back. A young librarian, a friend of mine, on taking up the book discovered at once—a thing I hadn't noticed—that two of the front (flyleaf) pages had been gummed together. He held them to the light and there was a name between them—perhaps that of the original owner.

EL PERRO Y LA CALENTURA, *Novella Peregrina,* etc. . . . What in the world is that? The Dog and the Fever . . . As she would lean over, the large reading glass in her hand, studying some difficult word, the scheme of what I had in mind began to unfold and I could secretly, under guise of taking down the translation take down rather her own words. It is obvious that she could not have told me all that is to follow in that way—but she told me enough—as I began to draw her out and the scheme developed—to which I add the notes I have taken for many years out of interest in her phraseology and way of thinking.

We sat mostly at her bedside using the sewing board she had won in some raffle at Waller's Department Store in the 1890's: That old thing, I got a prize from Waller's years ago, she said. She smiled when she told me where the board had come from.

Sometimes she would drive me almost crazy with her fumbling, and she would notice it and beg my pardon so that the cruelty in my voice from the exasperation of it would have to be cut short. It is very difficult for a younger person to deal with the aged—unless he be a saint. I was telling Vin the shoemaker about it this morning and he told me that one of his own kids had said, Dad, when you get old I'll let you take care of my furnace. He said it out of the kindness of his heart. I told Mother and she liked that.

Before us we usually had the Spanish-English Dictionary, a straight Spanish dictionary, my paper and pencils, her two or three pairs of glasses which she'd try one after the other according to the light, her reading glass and the text.

It's pretty hard, she said one day after she had had it a while preliminary to our getting started. It's like proverbs, in the old style. I have to guess at the words sometimes, they are not used any more. The sense is difficult to catch sometimes. It alludes to many things that have been forgotten.

How does it begin? I asked her.

It begins with two men walking in the fields and talking.

Oh yes, I said, *una novella peregrina*. Let's begin:

So we began. It served its purpose which was to draw out her comments. Let her come first, her childhood and early years, in her own words exactly as she told it.

Very seldom does a man get a chance to speak intimately of what has concerned him most in the past. This is about an old woman who had been young and to a degree beautiful a short number of years ago—this is as good a way as any to pay her my respects and to reassure her that she has not been forgotten.

An account taken from my mother's conversation while she was living with me at my home in Rutherford, New Jersey, during the years from 1924 to her death.

The French are always as if they had red pepper inside—
so quick. They don't care—

Caracoles—I have danced, danced—like a hurricane—
and they were always foreigners.

Oh, you ought to have heard Mrs. Wingwood tell when
my father was a young fellow. It was so funny, just as if
it had been yesterday.

Cher fils:
Je te prie de changer les "Liberal Bonds" tout de suite et de
mettre l'argent dans la Banque pour que je puisse payer le
plombier; toute la mécanique de l'eau marche bien maintenant.
Quel est le montant du peintre?

Au revoir,

Maman

R. H. Macy's
Please send C.O.D. a pair of sheepskin slippers to
snuggle cold toes—$1.34.
About the size of 4½ or 5 shoe.

Mrs. R. H. Williams

9 Ridge Road Rutherford, N.J.

Please send C.O.D. twenty 20 Christmas cards, small—

size ones and half of them saying greetings of the season.
Also a small bottle of liquid gum for scrapbook purpose.

Mrs. R. H. Williams, 9 Ridge Road
Rutherford, N.J.

That makes me go back (a rose-red verbena) when I
was eight years old. I had a little plant in a box.

I asked Mrs. L. to ask her husband if he would do it. I
mentioned it two or three times, but he didn't do it. You
wouldn't think there would be so many weeds so close to
the sea. It must have been a farm in the time.

All that will pass, the children, when they—
The tray: Your son has a head like *une lignotte*— Oh
yes, oh yes, he'd take it down!

Speaking of that, there was Émile Farline. He was a big
boy and they didn't give him a cent, not a penny. The
Farlines were like that, very stingy. Once he took some
money from his father's desk. I don't know how much.
They sent him to a sugar estate. Then they sent him to
Africa. He was a fine—looking boy about the age of Sonny.

My mother had funny ideas of her own—she would take
a piece of paper and stick it on the lamp where the light
would come in her eyes. I never saw anybody do that.

My mother used to sing in patois Français—

Ad el a ide
li ka fait la belle

> *li ka fait la belle*
> *li ka fait la belle*
> *Ad el a ide*
> *li ka fait la belle*

and she would laugh and laugh. My mother and father must have been like that. How? Oh, like to tell little stories to make you laugh. My mother used to play the guitar.

That must be some Indian or Japanese or something—they always have such funny things.

The Puerto Ricans have a way of saying—when something is uncertain—or not likely to happen—*a las viejos viruela.* (small pox to the aged)

—they tell each other—like the Spanish say: *botijuella verde.* (plain talk, or literally: green peas)

Did your boy come?
No.
I guess it's the warm weather—he likes to be cuddled up.

Looking at Florence I was thinking—so many Spanish people—that is—Spanish-speaking people—wear flowers in their hair—you know with black hair—a little flower—it's very nice.

Fifteen minutes! is a treasure to me these days.

Today just to pass the time, I was trying to remember all the people that there were in Mayagüez, when the

Dodds were living in Ponce. They were all foreigners. Merle de Lauris, very fine people. Mr. Merle was a tall man. I remember as a child I used to admire him, like a child, such a fine tall nice-looking man. Miss Merle married some Italian count. I can't remember his name. I was trying to squeeze my mind.

Paradis, Don Pepe Paradis. He owned an estate. Don Pepe and Isabel. Papa Paradis.

La Moutte et sa femme. They had the first school. The Grammar School. *Et son fils.* I can see a big woman like that, a French woman. Their son used to teach, he used to teach the piano too. It was he who would teach my brother little things. My brother was always crazy about music. M. Elie, that was the son, would teach him little things. Neither my mother nor my father knew. Then when he knew them he would play them at home. They bought him a little thing, I don't know. A harmonium? Like a little organ to work with his feet. He would sit there and play that.

Giacomaggi, a Corsican, had the high school for boys. For girls, before high school, it was El Señor Castro. He was from Venezuela, and Doña Pepita Castro, his wife.

Guenard & Mangual, they had a big sugar estate. Mme. Forestier—I shouldn't forget her. From the hacienda they had an alameda, an alley of trees, with mangoes on both sides. They used to call it the Restaurant of Mme. Forestier. All the boys and girls used to run there to pick up mangoes.

Lots of German comerciantes, business men. I only remember Mr. Krug, Mr. Lemmeyer and Mr. Wiggers—I don't know how to say it. And an Englishman, Mr. Wise. I used to run away there because they were good to me. You can imagine how small I was because I used to stand on his hand and he would lift me up and I could hold onto his head. Of course Toledo came a bit later.

I'm trying to remember the house. The street was called La Calle de Mendez Vigo. I don't think there was any number. That was the only street that went to the Plaza. The house had a big parlor, balcony in front toward the street, with two doors, French windows that opened to it. There was almost no front yard. Inside between the windows— I'm trying to remember everything I can—there was a big mirror. In front of that, so that the one who played it was with his back to the mirror, was an upright piano, and back of the piano, in the room, was the little organ that my brother played.

My father, it seems, was very fond of music. The piano, I remember, had two chandeliers on each side, of silver, which were taken out for Gottschalk to play—to give him more room. Patti was flying about and called my father Uncle. When Patti began to sing, she sang there. Patti was just beginning, a very young girl, my father brought her there, with Gottschalk. She was a very young girl.

To this side, to the left if you sit at the piano, was my mother's room and my crib was there. I suppose you call it a crib. It had high sides.

At the end of the parlor, to the back, in front of the hall, there were two folding tables with a door between them, with a silver candlestick on each—away from the French windows.

On the wall to the right was a life-size picture of my

mother, to the knees, and a black horsehair sofa with turned-up end. I remember I could slip myself there. In front of that was a table with books and a big lamp in the middle. On the other wall, opposite, my father's big picture, to the knees also. Once a week, I think it was once a week, those Germans would come and play cards and the tables at the back would be used.

The floor was of plain boards. You should see how they were scrubbed. No yard in front, a big yard in the back. There was a big *portón* that was never opened. You would come up the stairs, big steps, at the back to the hall and from there into the parlor. Then along the hall next to my mother's room there were two or three other rooms. Next to her room was a dressing room and a cabinet. Inside there was a big chair of dark wood and under it a big pot, because they had no toilet in those days. Then the other rooms. Then the dining room. Then the pantry where they had a barrel of flour, a barrel of molasses and pieces of meat, salt mackerel. There was a screened place to keep the cockroaches away. I can remember there were little plates with kerosene so that the ants would not climb in. Then the kitchen.

Last there was a steep pair of stairs, quite narrow, and there was the toilet that everybody used. Then going down the stairs, outside, there was a stable with a horse and under the kitchen a place where they had a carriage and the two colored men slept. Far at the back of the yard, there was sugar cane growing.

I can remember one of the colored men was Francisco. He had a trouble with his chest. What you call asthma. I can remember he used to have little turtles. I can see them so plain. He would cut their heads and drink the blood to cure him, I suppose. When I wanted to go somewhere and I could not go alone, Francisco would take me on his shoulder and I would hold onto his head and his neck.

A young woman in our church, Miss Prosh, an auto hit her, and now she's in the hospital with a broken pelvis.

The Spanish have a saying—shaking her finger in my face and raising her voice: *Malo, Malo, Malo, Malo! Si te conocia en el falo.* Bad, bad, bad, bad, if they know you in your weakness.

Machines? You heard about the little French old lady? They were talking about machines and they were saying they were going to make a machine to make the babies. And she said, No, I don't think so, I think the best way is the old natural way!

Visitor: I didn't want to stay any longer—so I made a ridiculous—How they say in Spanish? *un popel ridículo.*

Spanish proverb: *Aguanta cachete y calla porque si viene otro será peor.* Figuratively: A person that is punished and slapped saying to himself: Be silent and stand it, for if another comes, it will be worse.

On the 17th of September

Dear son Willie:

I have nothing material to send you, but:

I send you a garland of best wishes tied with love.

Mother

Gracious, how those girls disappeared! Young Louise had a fine voice—married an Italian—she was the youngest. They may be living on Long Island.

Odd bits of history amused her:

In 1777 nobody was sure which was the capital of the United States. The Congress retired when the English entered Philadelphia. The next day Lancaster was for a few hours the capital of the nation. Afterward it was removed to York. Then, the following cities were the capital of the United States: Philadelphia, Lancaster, York, Princeton, Annapolis, New York, and Trenton.

In 1855 John D. Rockefeller found his first employment as a clerk in a commission house in Cleveland, Ohio. He was sixteen years old and he was paid $3.50 a week. He economized from the first week; he had a few hundred dollars to invest when an opportunity came to him to buy a small petroleum refinery.

Twenty years after, the oil of the United States dominated the petroleum business. Today John D. Rockefeller is a multimillionaire.

You speaking that way makes me think of a little niece I had, Maria. She used to live with Alice. She had done something naughty and they told her that if she did that again, the *Bon Dieu* would punish her. *Oh, le bon dieu,* she said, *le bon dieu est à Bordeaux.* She didn't care. There was an image there, I suppose, that she knew.

A Contemporary:
As She Is: *Viellesse, félonne et fière—*
As She Was: (not a literal retreat)

Begins with an attack upon old age, what it does, what
it does to others—sclerosis—faces expressionless—the
mumbled word—

—and the mind, as if enclosed, signaling alive from
within—better than ever—ripened—every fault exagger-
ated, witnessed and unable to check it.

In Puerto Rico, in the country, they put the whites of
egg in a glass of water and next morning—if it form a ship
or a coffin—they believe in such things. (The day of the
dead)

She must have been bright, she must have been gay, with
a flash to her eyes—

When I was a child—children are very foolish you know,
and it can be dangerous. They wouldn't let me go—I don't
know any more where it was—with them. I took a little
piece of candle—

You don't know the story? It was one of those big
women who are very pompous and important. She was very
commanding and mean to her servants. When they
wouldn't do what she wanted them to do quickly enough,
she would slap them. So one day she died and the husband
of one of the women she used to slap all the time hated
her so much that, when he saw her lying there dead, he
went up to her and gave her a hard slap across the face.
But she had died suddenly and when he slapped her he
knocked a little bone that was sticking in her throat and

she came alive again. He must have been surprised when he
saw that, I can tell you.

Tutto è finito! Now it is just waiting.
Why don't you play the piano?
She showed me her hands. I can't make them go any
more. And this one drops down.

It's because I can't read. I want to see something, but
I can't see it. That tune is always in my head. I am saying
something, but I hear it there all the time. It makes me
crazy.

*She must be past eighty though she has been so secretive
about her age that no one knows really how old she is.*
Yes, I was born in December—but they always cele-
brated it in August. That was the only time they had Santa
Rosa. My name has always been crooked. They want to
know when I was born—keep asking me—they want to put
me with those, those . . . *que vayan freir munelos!* (Let
them go fry *munelos,* whatever they are!) Look at that,
that's for my birthday!
*We do know that she was ten years younger than her
brother Carlos, so as Albert says he would be past ninety
now, she must be past eighty.*
Now I remember my mother told me I was born between Saturday and Sunday. Or Sunday and Monday, I
don't know which: Halfway between, in the middle of
the night.
You were born on Christmas, weren't you?

Yes. Not Christmas. On the twenty-third or the twenty-fourth. I don't know!

1850?

We always used to celebrate the thirteenth of August. *Santa Rosa?*

I hated the name Rosa.

I tried other ways, asking how old a vase which she had brought with her from Puerto Rico was.

How old is it? I don't know. You know we never asked about those things. I am the Surropa. You know, what is left in the bottom of the bottle. I am the sediment. I am the last of the Mohicans.

Anyway, I am alive and old—and when I came here they told me, Oh that weather! It will finish you.

By the record in the Cathedral in Mayagüez, Puerto Rico, where she was born—Raquel Hélène Rose Hoheb lived to be one hundred and two years old! slightly more. I got it direct from the big book of the Recorder in the Mayor's office; he copied it out for me: Dec. 24, 1847.

He also uncovered the date of my uncle Carlos' license to practice surgery—he after whom I was myself named, with all the names of the petitioners certifying to his qualifications scrawled under it. To my great amusement and surprise I found also the license of my grandmother to drive her private carriage on the streets of the provincial city.

My mother had always told me she did not know when she was born but that it was close to Christmas. In fact it was on Christmas Eve, she was almost certain. Her uncertainty came from the fact that in Catholic countries,

especially in such a country as Puerto Rico, they cele-
brated their Saint's Day preferably to the day of their
birth. That, if she remembered correctly—and of course
she did—occurred in August, Santa Rosa her patron saint.
Birthdays for that reason meant little to her.

But 102 years! The record amazed me.

Beaufils was Spanish. That one that married Toto Longueville.

And Mrs. Lamb! I couldn't forget her. She was a great
friend of my mother. When she moved away she went to
St. Thomas. In St. Thomas on top of the mountain they
had a beautiful house. I suppose everything is burnt down
now. They had many fires. The piece of jewelry that Isa
took was from a wedding present Mrs. Lamb gave me. I
used to like to fix things up.

Once there was a fire across the street and my mother
took all her silver, her spoons and everything she had like
that and put them in a box. They came and told her that
she must leave the house quick, that the front was on fire.
When she went to look for the box, it was gone. She had a
woman who comes and tells where to find stolen things and
she told her the box was in the manure heap at the back
of the yard where they had hidden it until they could come
for it—but she had lots of people come; my mother believed in such things.

When Mt. Pelée exploded in 1902, the last of the Hur-
rards in America are supposed to have been blown to
eternity. So that the only ones continuing the blood are

*ourselves. They had a liqueur business in St. Pierre, so I
have heard the rumor. Very good stuff, though I had
never heard of it before—nor heard since: Hurrard & Cie.*

*The Monsantos, Enriquezes and Hohebs are all mixed
up in the telling about them. Apparently the Hohebs came
from Holland—Amsterdam most likely. Carlos tried for
years to locate some connection, or even to trace the name,
but without success of any sort. She remembers oil portraits
in Dutch costume. But Cousin Sissy hated old things and
all were lost or destroyed finally. Hoheb, the father, was of
a first marriage and the half brothers Enriquez were often
in his hair. How many generations there had been of them
in Puerto Rico and how they had mixed with the Spanish
there is completely lost.*

*And now she's still here—today at table we were speak-
ing of the cooking of rice. Floss was saying that she had
discovered that the brown rice we get is so much more
satisfactory than the white. The first time she tried it for
half an hour, then it was hard. The second time she cooked
it an hour, but it was still not quite satisfactory. Today
she cooked it two hours and it was just right, a little firm
but good. Mother said, that's the way they used to cook
it fifty or sixty years ago. They had a range, of course, and
put the rice on the back of the stove till it was properly
steamed. The poor people would eat nothing but rice and
beans, every day, every day,* arroz y habichuelas. *At home if
I had red beans Pop would always say,* Donde están las
habichuelas? *And imagine, Floss said, the Scandinavians
cook it in milk. Pugh!*

*It is pretty hard for her, but we get along a few pages
at a time. The thing isn't finished yet—we're about at page*

65 out of a possible ninety-six and neither one of us has read it through—but it's interesting in spots. And it gives me a chance to listen to her especially now when she is extremely limited in what she can say; I get a chance to take her in, all, a sort of limited comprehensiveness in what is really an extreme limitation: her room, the few papers she can decipher, a word or two of conversation.

The bitterness of old age, lameness, advancing cataract and the deafness of general sclerosis, of typical expressionless face that even alcohol can no more than flush and half arouse—past even the rancors of regret—old age is intensified by regrets that breed envy, resent solicitudes—

—finally quarrels with that which is nearest, flings what is in the hand aside careless of where it may fall—a sort of too tardy liberation—quarrels with its own infirmities at the last, bitterly.

Even tired of pretense to gain attention—comes out into a sort of clearing, what a man or woman might have been had he or she walked out simply into the street and existed. A horrible caricature of a life that might have been enjoyed, free of pretense, free of care or regret, free of restraint to the unvarnished truth of her condition. It is a discovery—so pathetically limited—

It is the limits that have made it possible, it is the awful finality of it that makes it uniform, universal and beautiful—and dreadfully sad to witness. The return of a sort of pride—real enough. It has a reflection for the brave world —one should know it. Life isn't complete without having witnessed it. It is the end of a life that has a sort of bony flower to the end.

She is beginning to get this, does not ask for a cure. Does not seem to mind any longer.

Trying to make up her mind whether to go upstairs for her hearing device—I wear it, but it does no good—Going halfway, wanting to turn back. Sitting. Then—I'll go up anyway. I'll put it on. I'll do something else.

Shall I bring you down again later?

With surprise and resentment, Why of course!—Very much awake and alert. The old pretense, hiding beneath it in order to gain an advantage. Waiting to be urged. The decay of infantile tactics. An apologetic insistence.

In the end the child itself—gradually—its happinesses and terror—still the decayed terrors of age:

How unfortunate.

She's an intelligent woman, but when she gets those bilious attacks she goes to bed in her own room. Yo prefiero morirse antes que tomar esas remedios de la botica! *(I would prefer to die rather than to take those drugstore remedies)*

Her son sends for the doctor, but she won't do anything. She prefers to take her own remedies, camomile and—You don't have those things here, she says.

That sounds like the old Puerto Rico!

Speaking of languages—When you Americans write Spanish, sometimes you forget.

—It was such a pity, just a month before I had to leave, the Russian girls wanted to teach me not Russian, but just the letters, so that I would know what they mean. Maria and Serafin. Such nice girls. Prohoroff. It seems that sometimes a little sign, a little mark over a letter makes it entirely a different sound in Russian. It is like that with the Spanish too. When foreigners write it at first, they sometimes forget to put in the little marks. Like the n. And it means something entirely different. Even a little shocking, if they want to write *año nuevo*, new year, they write *ano nuevo*—you know what that means? You know, behind.

Nunca digas de esta agua no beberas: Never say you will not drink of that water. (Never say never)
El que se hace de miel, se lo comen las hormigas: He who makes himself honey will be eaten by the ants.

I think the older I get the more I enjoy little children. They're like little birds, jumping around that way. They're so light and springy you know.

Yes, in the old days, in the West Indies, the servants always slept on the floor. They had a kind of mat, made out of—what do you call it?—Well, I suppose it's a kind of grass of some sort—they call them *petacka*—they unroll them on the floor and lie down there. You remember what happened to your father in Argentina. They took him to his bedroom and showed him the bed, very fine. But when he went to get in it, there was only a sheet spread over the wood. It was very beautiful but very hard.

By what my mother said, my father would never go to

those dramas. He said there was enough trouble in the world. He wanted to laugh and to be amused.

I was dreaming last night. It was a smooth plaster, like a hill. I don't know how I climbed up, but I did. When I was up there I could see a wall with letters on it. I said to myself, There must be people behind there. But when I went to go down I was afraid. I said to myself, I'll slip and fall. It was so smooth. I wanted to, but I could not. I was so frightened that I woke up.

You should say to yourself when you go to sleep that you will not be frightened, that it is a dream and that you will say to yourself, It is a dream. Then when you are up there, jump! just to see what will happen. You should not be so frightened. You must have been frightened sometime in your life. It is primitive fear.

I should say I have been frightened! I remember when my mother would go out, they would leave me with a colored woman. It was a two-story house near the town with a sugar plantation next to it, a big field. One night she was telling me how the Devil would come across the field and take little children up! I was listening with my very eyes. Then she told me to go upstairs alone to bed. I started up the stairs and the wind came across the sugar cane. Whooooo! I don't know how I got up the rest of the way. I fell to the top. I thought the devil had me for sure. They ran up after me and threw water in my face.

How it comes back to me! I can see my mother's big bed here and I had a little crib in the corner, there. At night I would be frightened and crawl over the sides very, very softly and into my mother's bed, near her. Many times she would wake and tell me, Go back to your bed. And I had to go back. It was cruel.

There was a girl that took care of a child I knew. She would want to go out to her lover, so she took some clothes and fixed them up in the room like a man. Then she told the child, If you don't go to sleep they will come and catch you. I can see the little child all curled up not daring to move.

They used to sing to me—strange how it comes back so clear! I can hear it singing . . . Elena! Elena! that was my name.

> Elena, Elena!
> El rey me quiere tener
> Niñito, niñito
> No te puedo defender

It was a little boy calling to his sister, Elena, Elena, the king is coming to get me. And she answered him, Child, child, I cannot help you.

When my father was sick—and he didn't believe in spirits or anything like that—all his friends were younger than he was—and one of them was called Alexandro de Castro, he was educated in Germany. This one had said good-by to my father and died on a ship at sea. There was a big room like this parlor, then there was a cabinet, and then the dining room on the other side. My father was looking and he said, Who is that young man sitting there? My mother thought it was somebody so she looked, but there was nobody there.

"Why there's Alexandro de Castro," said my father, "sitting there!" Father died like that! Quick. He was gone.

I remember—I don't know when it was—I was a young girl about fourteen years old—I must have been about that, somewhere around there. It was early in the morning, my mother was holding onto the other side of the door saying, *Mon Dieu, pitiez de nous, Mon Dieu, pitiez de nous, mondieupitiezdenous,* over and over again. I ran out, pfuit, past her (clapping her hands together like cymbals) in my nightgown out into the backyard and climbed on top of a big box that was there.

Earthquake?

Yes. And I remember once I had been bad at the table: I can see it so well. My father took his napkin, so, and struck me across the hands. How I screamed!

The fear that drives people out of their natures. The whole thing in a sense might be called the natural history of the fear that still wakes her screaming at night, then the vortex of that childish imagination.

I remember when I was a little child, I must have been very small because I was in my high chair. I suppose I must have been naughty for some reason because I can remember that my father took his napkin and twisted it so, between his two hands, and whipped me with it. Then he called Thomasina—she was a big colored woman whom we had, we used to call her Mamita, she would be angry if

you didn't call her that—and Thomasina took me in her
arms to the kitchen. I remember I tried to kick and to bite
her, but she took my own finger and put it in my mouth
so that I bit it hard, and I remember it!

*In the end the child itself—gradually—its happinesses
and terror—still the decayed terrors of age:*

*Terror even of her bones, never having broken them
except in very old age. How unfortunate.*

My mother used to comb my hair straight back with a
comb at the back to hold it. Agh, *chivo!* She would call me
a goat, she said I looked like a goat.

That makes me think—I used to see my mother, when
I was a child, playing cards at night on the table. They
were like in a square and she would change them, one here
one there all around. They called it Reuscite, I think. It
had a meaning—each card meant something. I think the
queen of spades meant death. Like that. Sometimes it
would come out and then it meant you would be very
successful in anything you wanted to do.

It is as if I were another person now—what I was then.

This "Contemporary" is my mother—
Raquel Ellen Rose Hoheb
whose mother was
Meline Hurrard
of Martinique and
whose father was
Solomon (I think) Hoheb,
half brother of the Enriquez of ??

Kruger, Isobel or whoever it was stole the ring and the small hacienda—alike. The fear this brought to the child— my mother. The natural instincts of the child unable to cope with the natural history of human avarice—it still wakes her screaming at night.

Carlos was the first and he lived, of course, but then there were five or six others, all of whom died in infancy. Then she came. Just Carlos and she. Naturally she looked up to him and he spoiled her along with the others, but there were ten years between them and that made a special difference and the old man had died.

If I hand her her cane—perhaps carelessly and she misses her grasp and drops it—she goes into a minor fit: Oh stupidity! she says, blaming herself. There's a luxury in self-accusation which had better not be indulged in for too long a time. She should have outgrown it.

I left that rose for you to see. Isn't it beautiful? and smell it.

flabjock: flapjack

I ate too much, I feel—*pough!* It makes me think of the story of the big Negro. It isn't very nice. It happened at the time of the fiesta around Christmas or New Year's perhaps. He ate too much, and drank too much. I can't speak *patois:* Especially he drank too much. *Grand Coucou Grappe! Grand Coucou Grappe!* I suppose he meant like a cup made of half a coconut you know. *Et puis mou bois, mou bois, mou bois.* And he was very sick. They asked him why he did it and he replied, *C'est na ponitesse! C'est na ponitesse!* Finally he took himself off to the river—I wish I could speak the *patois: Et, puis mou caca, mou caca,* etc., etc.

(I drank) (it was just politeness) (and then I shat, etc.)

Oh! Oh! That leg is a mystery

One day sitting in the dark—she took a great interest in the bakery across the street—she said she could see a basket in the window, but she couldn't make out what it had in it, thought they were buns. And in the florist's window next door there were purple flowers in a vase. She had been amusing herself with a pair of opera glasses watching whatever there was to see in the street.

I thought, what's the use, so I stopped writing. Since then, I have had three letters—she waited for every boat, she thought something had happened—so now I will write again. If she had what she used to have—but now she has no room. Or else I could go. But you don't know how old people get. You haven't experienced that yet. We like our things that we are used to, to have our own place and the things we like. We don't want anything new any more. We want to be with our own things.

If my mother were alive, I would tell her: Well, I am too *la virgen de los siete dolores.* (the virgin of the seven pains)

Her convinced child's voice: Oh well. Beginning like that, I have to finish like that. I can't change now.

Speaking of the latest popular craze in songs—The music goes down and around—Floss was saying she saw them putting coal in across the street and the man on top of the load was singing it at the top of his voice, completely ignoring every one else on the avenue. I got the words now, he was saying to his helper. Then he'd sing it so you could hear him a block away.

That reminds me, we had a boy, in those days, whose feet were all swollen—from what you call—elephantiasis, yes that's it, so that he couldn't put on shoes. But he had a talent for music. He would imitate everything. On Thursday afternoon—the band of the regiment that was there would give a concert in the Plaza. And he would go there all by himself and listen. Not the cornet—Yes the clarinet perhaps. Then he would come home and whistle the whole thing. He would sit there and whistle so that the people would stop on the street and listen to him. His name was Enrique. He used to clean the knives. And take care of the horse. That was another thing. He loved horses. He would sit in front of the house with his eyes shut and tell you every horse that would pass in the street.

You know the knots that come in a piece of wood. When you take one from a board it looks like a horse's hoof. He had a whole collection of them and he would take them in his hand and make the sound of a horse—all kinds of imitations. Poor fellow, I suppose he's dead now.

And there was a musician called Tamares. He was a graduate of the conservatory in Paris. In that time they had those beautiful contra-dances. There were five men who would be in the shoemaker shop and they would make the dances. They would imitate all the instruments and invent new tunes. Tamares would go there and write them down for them. Many of the dances came from that shoemaker shop.

I think I'll close that window. It might happen—what when you're not here it might come in (I closed it). There. Now that's done. "Cabas done", like the St. Thomas Creoles call it.

Speaking of strong men. My father's brother—Of course, I don't know anything about my family. I only know what they told me. He was very muscular. Once he had an argument with one of his employees. He got so angry he took the man by the seat of the pants and held him out of the window and told him: If you say another word, I'll drop you.

They say he would let three men take hold of a cord and he would take the other end and pull them all around.

By the way, I just heard from Albertito that Alfred Christi had just died at the age of ninety . . . ? And he wouldn't have died then if he had not fell down and broke his leg.

What, climbing trees to get fruit?

No, he was too old for that. I remember he used to chase

the young girls. He would kiss them. They used to run like the dickens. The Christi sugar estate was next to our house and when I was a little girl I used to go there without any shoes and sit under a guava tree. I would gather my skirt full of fruit and eat them. I would eat the green ones first and save the best. Then when I came to them I couldn't eat any more. Mangoes I would eat like a pig until my whole face was yellow with the juice up to my eyes. Just like a little pig.

They have guavas—but those they don't cook—exactly the same shape and the same color as a pear. They call it the pear guava. It is kind of whitish inside, not red like the others. They say when you plant an apple seed in the tropics it comes up a guava. I don't know if it is true.

The guava you find growing more in the country, like a plum. Yes, they eat them raw—they are very good. The mango they plant in yards like our apple trees or peach trees. I remember there was a whole double row of them at Mme. Christi's along the road leading up to the hacienda, the boys coming home from school would pick them up from the ground. Then there is the *caimito*. It is round like an apple and bright green, but inside it is pure white, like milk. Toledo always called me *cara de caimito*, because when I was young my face was round like that. The *nispero* is about the same size only it is brown and soft inside— fluffy. They say:

> El que nispero come
> y esparrago chupa
> bebe cerveza
> y besa una vieja

ni come, ni chupa
ni bebe, ni besa

> He who eats the nispero
> and chews asparagus
> drinks beer
> and kisses an old woman
>
> neither eats, nor chews
> nor drinks, nor kisses

When a child eats the *caimito* he must be a little careful because the inside near the skin sticks all around the mouth all white and you cannot get it off, it is like glue.

Then there is the *corazón*, red and shaped like a heart, and the *quenepas*, small like a plum and green, it comes in bunches and you bite it and open it, tac! and suck the inside. It leaves a pit that rattles inside the skin when you shake it. There is a bean too, the *guama*, that, when you open it, has little things like cotton and inside of each is the seed. It is very sweet. You take each one out and suck it. There is, too, a grape that grows by the sea, a seaside grape. But it is different from the grapes here. It is more the shape of those torpedoes that the children throw down, tac! and they explode. They are pinkish and very good.

Strange how we remember the things when we were children—and not afterward. I used to cry when they wanted to send me to school, so my mother hired a carriage. There were four little girls. The driver's name was Anaclito, he was a good-natured man. Then there was a steep bank where there was a fruit called *algaropa;* I must see what that is in English. It is hard like a rock, the color of mahogany and shaped like a pea pod. We used to beg him to stop the carriage. We would promise to embroider him a pair of slippers or we would promise him a handkerchief or anything. He would smile and stop for us to get down. Then we would take that fruit. No decent person would eat them. You would have to crack them with a stone. And inside there was a dry, dry powder. But dry, dry! We would eat this. It was kind of sweetish. When you chew it, it would get like mud. Awful! But we would enjoy that. It would stick to your mouth.

That makes me think—children are so funny. When I was a little girl we used to eat what they call *cerezas*, cherries. They had one seed inside and they were sour, sour! They were a yellow color. We used to try to see who could eat the most without making a face and I used to win. I would eat five or six until I could no more. They are not really cherries, they have marks on them like a melon—but they are the same size as cherries here.

It's snowing—in April!
Snowing?
Yes.
I suppose just a little. Just to show there's a little left in the bottle.

Run, run, run, run, run, run!
That's it.
—but if you don't go you can't eat.
—you can't dress, you can't go *any*where.

I don't know what the Caracanos mean when they say:

De los parientes
Ni los dientes!

I suppose not to expect anything from relatives. Of course there's no rule without exception.

El que se mete a redentor sale crucificado.
(He who wants to be a redeemer ends up crucified)

As a little girl I can remember those cousins of mine dressing and wiping the perspiration. Anita would never dry.

Maybe it was the salt in her.

Yes, maybe.

When I arrived at Puerto Plata there was a young American—what was his name?—he gave me a song. "If its a dream, Let me dream again"—a very pretty song. What was his name? I had it just now. Funny how it goes like that. Oh yes, Mr. Gould—he was very nice looking and he could sing too.

Like the servant when they reprimanded her so much. *Mais, Madame, j'étais fait comme ça.* (But, Madame, that's the way I am made)
Pansies in a letter
from my mother—
shall we say
that they are roses
fresh with dew?

In Puerto Rico the bride borrows a ring and the bride-groom a jacket, and so they get married.

They bring their dead in those palm—it isn't a leaf—they tie them in there and bring them to be buried—

—they used to come to beg on one day in the week—I think it was Wednesday. They would say *un alemito para este pobre.* Then you would give them a penny or a piece of codfish or anything. There was one woman who used to have a paralyzed arm—loose like that. We used to make fun at her—children are cruel—I was among them. My mother used to comb my hair straight back with a comb at the back to hold it. Agh, *chivo!* She would call me a goat, she said I looked like a goat.

I smell the stew. It makes me think of Mrs. Hope. She never could understand why Pop objected to the smell of cabbage cooking—in the house. She liked it. It smells so good, she said.

When my mother was in America, before she had any children—perhaps it was when she was first married, she said she remembered a big river. And that you didn't dare say you were Catholic. They weren't wanted here.

When I was baptized I had a ribbon around my waist all with little gold pieces on it—and when I was older they gave me a whistle—of silver I think, with bells around it.

va comme je te pousse (go as I push you)

Mas vale caer en gracio que ser gracioso
(better to stumble into grace than to be a clown)

They had a parrot and they didn't want him to eat *habichuelas*—I don't know why—they told him it would make him bald. So when anyone would come that was bald he would say: *Comiste habichuelas, comiste habechuelas!* (You ate beans! You ate beans!)

She brought me that, I don't know what they are, some kind of branches with flowers. She's a true person, you can rely on her. She is honest. Her little daughter has a face like a balloon. And have you seen her skin? It is hard to paint a skin like that. It is easy to paint an ugly person or with defects. Paul has a friend that comes here. Have you seen him? He has a kind of yellowish skin and beautiful eyes. If he was in France, they would catch him. A fine face to paint. But a little face like that—it is very hard.

When people come in the afternoon like that I don't do anything. Just talk—about nothing at all. In Puerto Rico, the natives call it *hablando caballo*—horses' talk.

My mother used to tell a story—she had stories to tell—about two old women like that (pointing to a picture of two old women talking together, in the *Geographic Magazine*). You know how in the Spanish countries they do like that (showing) with the thumbnail on a tooth, to say they have nothing at all. One of them was saying, I haven't got *that!* making the gesture. She only had one tooth and she couldn't find it in time. I haven't got—But she couldn't find the tooth—not even the tooth.

Christmas, 1932

During the holidays the Hibaros would come—but the real people from the country. Sometimes one man and two or three women, sometimes not so many, sometimes more, and they would stand there and sing their songs, in their own language. The *gurano*—to keep time, and the women with their handkerchiefs on their heads would sing. One song I remember, but they had many songs—their own *chi, chick chie, chickie chie*—one song was—

Año nuevo

Reyes

Pascuas y

Nacimiento—they come and go, but we are always here.

I was told that in the olden days those Hibaros were quite brave. When they used to fight—with machetes—they would get tired and sit down and fight that way too.

Then the real African from the plantations, the true Negroes would come too—with their *bambrilo*—and dance, jumping up and down. I remember one man he had on a kind of skirt of grass. I don't know what he had under it—but he would jump there. All that is in my head like yesterday, but it is funny I can't remember my father's face.

Once I don't know what happened, but the Negroes were dancing and singing and my father took his stick. I tell you they ran downstairs and out of the house.

There was an idiot that came in a long shirt, he was a real idiot, but he was wicked enough to know when there were women and girls there—and he would lift up his shirt.

Strange all that is in my mind.

We used to consider it a *great* privilege when they would allow us to take the chicken bones and eat them in the backyard, outside. Two little friends—Terecita Turul and Marguerita Marana. I must have been very small then.

When your father was coming to the house, making love, my brother said to me: He's a nice fellow, but he still wears rings.

He used to come every day, every day, every day. So one day around six o'clock we saw a man coming with a trunk. Your grandma was like that all her life. She sent his trunk after him.

How would you say in English? How would you translate it?

Y esta es aquélla? (And this is she?)

Y esto es aquél? (And that is he?)

It was two who used to be lovers. They were going each with a friend and they passed the one they had been in love with years before. And he said to his friend: *Y esta es aquélla?* He couldn't believe it. And she said too: *Y esta es aquél?* You couldn't translate that into English without a long sentence explaining what it was.

Gracious, how those girls disappeared. Young Louise had a fine voice. Albertina married an Italian, she was the youngest. They may be living on Long Island. I wonder if you have a telephone directory where we could find their names. Bath Beach—somewhere there.

In Spain when they would have a religious procession—
the way they used to be—everyone would take off his hat
when the Saint was passing. I forget which one it was. But
this man was walking with his chest out and his hat on. He
was a carpenter, I suppose—the one that made the figures
out of wood.

Take off your hat, they said to him, see the Saint is
passing. But he swaggered and paid no attention to them.
He merely said: *Yo lo connosi ciruelo. Ciruelo* is a plum
tree. He meant he knew the figure—or the Saint—when he
was still a tree.

When your father used to travel with Mr. Kemp—one
day in Paris, I think, he said, Well, Williams, we're going
to have a fine dinner today!—He had received a little
barrel of fine corned beef from New York. He was going to
have corned beef and cabbage.

Have the English something else to say that a woman is
an old maid? In Spanish they say, *Se quedo para vestir
santos.* And in French they say. *Elle va coiffé la Sainte
Katherine.* Any girl that was past twenty-five was considered an old maid. And on the feast day of St. Katherine
they would all celebrate. They have nothing like that in
these times. It was considered a disgrace in Spanish countries for a girl to work, so the father kept them at home.

There was a big fellow—he was young though—just like
a boy—a Scotchman—used to go with my brother—and

talk. Light . . . Lightboy. No. Lightbody—that was his name.

There were two sisters in Paris; one was smart and the other was stupid. The smart one had just finished reading a book. She said to her sister. "Ask me any question about that book, anything at all—open it and ask me and I will tell you what it says." The stupid one took the book and opened it. "Can you answer any question that I ask you about it?" "Yes," said the other. "Very well then," said the sister: *"Eh bien, qu'arriva-t-il ensuite?"*

(Well, what happened then?)

Le bleu domine! so she went to the paint store and asked for *le bleu domine.*

(She thought *le bleu domine* was a color.)

Son, I have been thinking of that woman. If that's the worst of her insanity, to give things, you should be patient with her. Tell her quietly she mustn't do so much.

Yes, I said, but if she gives away and spends so that her husband and her family suffer, then it's not so funny. Besides, she wears them out with her constant activity which is not normal.

Well, the poor thing . . . that, yes, is too much. It makes me think of an old couple in France, in a town I have forgotten a long time ago. He was a little crazy, I think he used to drink. His wife kept a little store and one day when she was away for a few hours he sat in front of the store and called the people. "Here," he said, "take this." And he would give them something. And so, he had given away almost all the things which were for sale. When she came back, there was nothing. Since it was in a small town the people brought most of it back. But I suppose she must have lost something.

"Oh! look at the fruit!" (a pushcart full of bananas).
"Oh! look at the fruit!" (a stall full of apples in baskets).

I think I would have been a good portrait painter I like so much to study faces.

In Mayagüez, where I was born, they were all foreigners: French, English, Germans. That was where I first heard the name, Willie. My mother was a godmother to Willie Lamb, whose mother was English. The Germans were unmarried and they all lived together in a house which was called *"la casa de los Allemanes."* They never called it anything else. They came to work in the sugar and the coffee plantations up in the mountains. Some of the typical names were Christi, Merle, and Lamb. It was cool in the mountains. They even had strawberries.

I was reading about Pavlova in one of your papers. I didn't know she was dead so long, about a year. They say she had an absolutely perfect body, feet and everything— but perfect. I always feel sorry when someone who is doing so nicely here in the world has to die.

10/16/32
(The new maid) Not a bad girl, *la petite.* Not a bad fault to be very clean. Like my grandmother who used to slap

the little colored servant and then go and wash her hands afterward. *Au moins quand elle finit une chambre c'est bien fait.*

Picture of tropical shore—beach:
—you see this is a little part of the sea—secluded. The ladies go to bathe there. Near Mayagüez.

A little song I used to sing when I was a young girl—it has been running in my head all day. It makes me think of Coquelin, the only time I saw him. It has to be Coquelin to tell it. He had a song in his head and he couldn't get rid of it. But you would have to see him to understand. Nobody could be so funny. Finally he jumped into the water to drown himself to forget the obsession. When he came up vomiting the water out of his mouth—the song was still there.

Oh yes—let me see:

> *Por ti mi dulce Sylvia*
> *Por ti lo pierdo todo*
> *El mundo entero si me mandas*
> *Me strebo a conquistar*

—I was a very young girl. I suppose it is *"mandas."* The last is funny *"me strebo a conquistar."* You can imagine.

> (For you my sweetest Sylvia
> For you I foreswear all
> The whole world if you command it
> That I strove to subjugate)

They had a dog in Puerto Rico—and they called him: *Yo no say.*

(I don't know)

The night is my *kokora,* oh dear—because I don't get a position

She be like her grandfather, he cough like that all him life and he live to be one hundred and three years old.

To her leg: Now you behave a little better tonight.

Yes, there was some famous actor, a comedian, who was feeling sick and he went to a doctor who told him: There's nothing the matter with you. What you need is to forget yourself. Go out, go to the theater, see so and so. He will make you laugh.
But doctor, replied the patient, I am that man.

L'art? C'est aspect prochain de l'esprit eternele.
(Art? it is the living spirit of all that is eternal.)

When Godwin went to get Mr. Hubbard with the little old carriage we had, huh, he was afraid he wouldn't get home. You know it kept pounding so, boom, boom—on the springs. Yes. That's too much, three hundred pounds. He was so tall, too.

Little Marie Pratt—she was funny. When she went to visit tante Alice they tell many things about her. Once she was naughty and Alice told her: *"Le bon dieu te punira si tu fais ça."* Marie replied: *"Oh, le bon dieu, le bon dieu,—le bon dieu est à Bordeaux."*

(God will punish you if you do that. *Le bon dieu, Le bon dieu,* is in Bordeaux)

And once Marie saw tante Alice dressing and she noticed the hair under her arms. She was completely astonished. *Oh tante Alice, tante Alice,* she said, *tu as des ailes.*

(You have wings.)

File Ellen!
ou crains
ma colère.

Ernestine de Keratriz, my friend when we were little girls, she made it up. I don't know what she meant.

Dr. Preto, in St. Thomas where your grandmother lived so long, he didn't mind what he said either. He was a type. He had a long white beard and white hair. He used to go in a low carriage and everyone called him father—all the little children. Oh well, he would say, maybe they are right, perhaps it is true, it may be.

January

Dear Doctor:

I have not yet thanked you for the great kindness you had to come to see me and to give your advice.

Mr. Gubitosi brought the pair of shoes he made for me two weeks ago; they don't fit right: too wide, too long, consequently friction on the toes, and the big hard box by the end of the shoes will make me stumble; I do not like it. Mr. Gubitosi says he cannot make any alteration without your order.

However he is paid already, but I may order for another pair.

With thanks to you doctor,

Yours sincerely,

*That was when Anna was there, she was an awful nice
girl. I remember when Papa was coming from South America, she fixed all the dining room—she put green branches
on the chandelier and all around on the walls—everywhere.
And she took a branch of apples from the tree by the
kitchen and hung it by a string to the wall. There must
have been at least six big apples hanging on it. They
stayed there for a month drying up. She was an awfully
nice girl. You remember that old German who used to
come around and bother us for work. She fixed him. She
told him* pan pan vino vino. *(Bread, bread, wine wine: or
the facts of life.) He never came back any more after that.*

I would like to know why the French always put that line
like a "t," on the seven.

Lucky! I should say they were—those two girls. Like the
Spanish say: They didn't have a place to drop dead.

(dessert) Have a sigh! In Spanish they call those *suspiros*.

How people remember sometimes. *Stupid* things that
happened. My brother used to remember that when he was
a little boy my mother sent him with a servant to get a
pitcher of molasses to eat with something. He was so
happy he was jumping up and down and his head hit the
bottom of the pitcher in the servant's hand. It went all over
his head. He never forgot it.

When people are going to die, they always do something
funny. I think I told you about my father. He *always*
wanted to do something funny. One time he was very sick

in bed. I think it was Madame de Longueville—she was so fond of my mother, and my father. She always would want to do something for them. Her favorite was to send a rice pudding. My father used to say: "I think we have sub-scribed to that." They say he always wanted to make people laugh. This time he was very sick in bed and there were a lot of women in the room talking and whispering. So he started to get up, you know how they used to have a com-mode in the room, and all the women ran out. Then he started to laugh and got back into the bed. I didn't want to go there, he said, he just wanted to be quiet; they bothered him.

Once, many years ago, Luisa Frascheri was here. She was cooking rice and I saw her put a teaspoonful of vinegar in it. I don't know why.

My brother he used to like to eat well—he wasn't a *gourmand* but a gourmet. When he would eat at table he would say sometimes, I could go to a banquet now and eat everything from the beginning.

Speaking of that—huh! Jeanne Farine always used to say: *J'ai une fuite dans le dos!* (I have a stabbing pain at the back.) I don't know what she would mean. Poor girl, she's dead now.

Il faut que je prenne a little *pildorito.*
(I have to take a little pill)

I was telling her about César Franck—what kind of a

*man he was and how some of the members of the Sorbonne
made excuses so they would not have to go to his funeral:
That makes me think, she said, about a Frenchman who
bought the candles for his own coffin—and put fireworks
inside. When he was dead and they went to light them it
went Shooooooo!*

That big fat servant you had here, one morning she
brought me too much oatmeal. I told her it was too much
—but she left it anyway. And I ate it after all. When she
came up for the tray, she looked and she said, "Well, I see
you got away with it." I thought that was so funny.

It was like—I have never forgotten it. It was that little
shoemaker across the track where we used to go. There was
a little boy who was thirsty and he got him a drink of
water. And he said to him, "That's right, pitch in, my son,
pitch in." It struck me very strange.

And I remember too, Juliette Monsanto, when I first
came here. I knew some words, but no more than that. She
used to say "boid" instead of bird. And she would say,
"What a cheek!" I remember how it impressed me.

That was where I lost my solitaire. They swiped it.
Tocar el piano à reves, the Spanish say. (Play the piano in
reverse)

It isn't that I'm namby pamby, no sir, I can fight like
anything—I am impetuous. But I have dominated myself
—like iron.

When I was first married—just when I was married, you

might say, and your father was so ill and had to be operated on. She wouldn't let me into the room. When I would get in, just to look sometimes, she would come and say, "You mustn't go in, he is sleeping!" I tell you I have been good in my life. Sometimes I could have taken her by the neck and strangled her.

It's a pity you didn't.

Yes, perhaps sometimes—But one day I slapped her with all my strength—It was better after that.

We were all timid, my family. Once, when my brother was at school in France, every Sunday he would go to Mme. Farine and eat for the week. So one day he came a little late and dinner was finished. He had had no breakfast so as to eat more—and when they asked him he said no, he was not hungry. I tell you he suffered that day, he said he felt pain all the afternoon—he could hardly stand up. The food at the school was so bad he couldn't eat it.

In the time of the Gauls, speaking of that now, when they had a feast, the bravest of the men would have the leg—to hold in his hand I suppose. If it was a chicken or an animal I don't know which, he would have the leg for himself. And if there were two, then they would fight to see who would have it. But for real. Until they would kill each other sometimes. Imagine! For a thing like that. Such a little thing they would kill each other. Stupid! In the time of *los barbaros*.

And the men were everything. The women and children had nothing to say. A man could kill his wife and his child too if he wanted to. He owned them.

Only in one thing did the women have anything to say. That was the one thing they did right. When it was a girl and she was old enough to marry, they would have a feast. She would sit there and her father would invite all the young men, all those who could be her husband to come there. And she would choose: Nobody else had anything to say. Just she. She would go to the one she wanted and present him with a little pitcher—I don't know what you call it—an *acceuille*—with a narrow neck. Like that. And he would be her husband.

But as soon as they were married, then he could do anything. He could kill her just the same. And if she had a baby, you know sometimes if she was in love with someone else, and he suspected it. As soon as the baby was born, he would take it to the river and put it with everything around it, on his—his *bouctier*. Hollow like that. Yes, his shield and let it go floating on the river. I suppose it would drown.

Ah, I said, that accounts for so many knights and ladies who used to go wandering in the forest. I suppose some peasant, some woodchopper, would find it floating there and say, Hm, that's a pretty good looking kid,—and take it and bring it up.

Yes, but if it was his own child, they would fix it all up nicely and bring it to her.

I used to make monkey faces. I was the champion monkey face maker. Gracious! I can see all those people; Jacobo used to have the tears running down his face from laughing. But he went crazy afterward. My mother used to hide her face, but she was laughing just the same. *Elena! la cara larga,* she would say, you mustn't do that, you will spoil your face.

When I was a child I wanted so much to play the castagnettes. But there was nobody to teach me. They did send me a pair from Spain: Isobel de Hiberga, the intimate friend of my mother.

Just when I'm giving him a bath, he decides to do one thing or the other.

Carramba! I forgot to cut my nails. I'm just like *un galivan.* (alligator)

There was a Spanish doctor when we lived in Puerto Plata, who practiced there. But he had nothing to do, everybody wanted my brother. So he boarded at our house. I mean he took his meals there—three times a day for many months. Rita was furious at him because he never paid—he had no money—for months at a time.

I painted his portrait, a full sized figure—but three-quarter length. It was very good, they said. I would like to see it now. I cannot remember his name. Rita would know. He used to bring me a bottle of white rum. You would put in it those jasmine, that's it, and when you took a bath you used it. It would perfume the whole room.

It is as if it were another person now—what I was then.

Manuel Enriquez was another. He came to our house for a few days and stayed three years. That's how I came to know him so well. Then just when he went away, my father died. He could eat too, he liked his meals!

No hay mal que dure cien anos. Ni cuerpo que lo resiste.
(There is no evil that lasts a hundred years. Nor body
which can bear it)

Crazy: *Unos por poco lo son y unos por poco no lo son*
(Some lack little of being so and others lack little of not
being so.)

There was a German fellow who used to come around
and sell vegetables and fruits from a cart. You must excuse
me if I tell you this. Grandma was looking at the vegetables
and she held up one of the boys, I forget which one it was,
she held him up in her hands and said: Look, look! How
would you like to have one of these? No thanks, replied the
man, my machine is still good.

Macaque connait que bois li monter:
(Monkey knows which tree to climb)

*Mother had a thin gold bracelet decorated with an acan-
thus leaf scroll either side of the center—and fastened at
the ends as though it were of leather, with a pin and holes.
It was so thin and flexible. On the framed oblong in the
center in script letters was the legend:* Tacet.

Seeking to get another to pay his bill—she found herself
doubly saddled: *El tiro sallio por la culeta.*
(The shot back fires—out of the breech)

Mon dieu (getting up from table) *je suis sale comme un
peigne.*

(Mon dieu, I am filthy as a comb)

Pst! *Bête va,* as Ludovic used to say.
(You Clown)

To the cat: There's nothing now. Do you smell anything? Nothing at all. You're not so fat now, you're not so
fat as you were.

Moro viejo, mal Christiano
(Old Moor, make a poor Christian)

How one thing makes you think of something else.
When you did that, it made me think of one of my old
friends. There were two sisters, they were my intimate,
intimate friends. Once Ernestine did that: *Brrrrrrup! Vive
la République!* Paulina was more like her mother, Madame de Keratry. I wonder what has become of them, if they
married and had children and if they went to the war. Perhaps they were killed. Who knows?
  (In derision, after a belch: Vive la République!)

He must have been the black sheep of the family. He
went to Caracas—I was young. I was not interested in politics and all that. He became a General in the Army of
Venezuela. Then he married a woman from down there. I
suppose he had to leave the country after a while. He came
to Mayagüez. The two girls were my own age and we were
intimate friends.
  Then after some years he felt that he wanted to go back
to France and I lost track of them for years.

But when I went to Paris one day I was riding on the trolley car and a man came up to me and said, "Is this Elena Hoheb?" It was Monsieur de Keratry. He took me at once to the family, to the Countess. They treated me like a daughter. They were delighted to have me there. I could have stayed to do what I wanted to, to paint. They did not want to let me go. But I was ashamed. Later I was sorry. But I did not want to go to them like a beggar that way.

He would tell me what to say to his mother, to please her. That is what I mean, a friend. He would say to call her *Ma petite Mère*. So I did. She liked it. It pleased her.

They lived in winter on the Boulevard St. Germain. Of course, in summer they would go to Lancy. But here they had a big garden. The gardener would bring in a big bouquet of flowers every day.

Mme. de Keratry would say, *Mes enfants, maintenant il faut chanter*. Then we would have to play the piano and sing. Or she would say, *Mes enfants, maintenant il faut vous promener*. Then we would have to go for a walk.

It was she who gave me the locket, the one which Florence has now: they wanted to do everything for me. Once they had a grand supper and I was to be there. Oh, they were very *collet monté*. Mme. de Keratry said to me: you must do this, you must do that. You must not put your arms on the table. They were all nobility. It was a very fine affair. So, of course, I had to be somebody so they could introduce me. So M. de Keratry introduced me as, *la soeur du plus grand médécin de Puerto Rico*.

(The sister of the most famous doctor of Puerto Rico)

For this dinner, she bought me the materials for a dress and had it made too, beautifully. It was pongee silk with little ruffles of lace all over. Very finely made.

It was beautiful the way they lived. *Mes enfants, maintenant il faut aller à l'église.* And they would give us each two sous. So funny. On Sunday afternoon the Curé would come. I can see him, a fat little man. He would come to play cards with the Countess.

(Children, now we must go to church)

It makes me think, it was a man in some amateur theatricals. He had forgotten his lines—he was playing the part of a count—so when he didn't know what to do any more, he said: *Se murio il conde,* and fell down on the floor.

(The count is dead)

November 10, 1930

At the bridge: *Carrambita, carrambole*—just in time, just in the nick of time! *Carrambita, carrambole.*

What is that? (A small group of cars stopped at a traffic sign) I am as bad as the Frenchman, when he first came to this country: he thought it was an accident—by the ferry.

Your car needs sweeping, child.

It was funny about the holdup, two doctors and a nurse were in it. I suppose they hushed it out.

Every morning when I wake and see the sun, I am learning that poem and I try to remember it.

I like that last line: *La terre salut l'astre du jour et de l'amour.*

(the earth salutes the day star and the star of love)

Castellar—39, q'es eyo che, I don't know what it is.

Corneille, yes, that was his name. Les Horace, it was. I used to recite a piece from that—they would always give me the dramatic things to do:—*Rome, enfin que je hais!* D'Archambeau would make me sing, *L'adieu de Marie Stuart.* Always the dramatic.

A Coronet of Weeds: (title)

Caracoles! I used to dance, like a hurricane and always with foreigners.

Esos son historias, musica celestial
(those are mere lies, celestial music)

I think I'll close that window.
Yes, do. It's very funny, any change affects me. I may even be sleeping and, if it gets very hot, I wake up right away. Or, if it gets cold, it's the same thing. I suppose my nerves are very sensitive, anything affects me. I am not a person any more, but I still have some use as a barometer— when it is cold my pains are much worse.

Won't you have a cigarette, Mother. Really, you ought to learn to smoke, it would do you good, it would quiet you down.
No. I don't want to. Once when I was a girl they told me

that if I cleaned my teeth with a cigar it would make them strong and white. So I took a cigar and rubbed them with it. Well, before breakfast. Chah! I was sick as a dog after.

The Spanish have a saying—I must have told you, *Haciendo de tripas corazon*—that is, when you have no heart for anything, make it from your bowels.

I want to go up now, I feel a little tired. It's getting worse and worse.

But even in the honesty of her complaint there is an air of impatience with herself—a self accusation. The traces of a self-indulgence which she has never outgrown are apparent in the way she blames herself for things that require no apology.

To her leg: Now you behave a little better tonight. *Va comme je te pousse* (go as I push you).

In Mayagüez, where I used to live, when they wanted to call you a pig, instead of saying—*asi esta tu*—they would say, *asi esta brrrrrrp,* making a noise like a pig. I can't do it now.

Yes, said she, I know what you mean. There was a man like that in Mayagüez, such a talker. My brother would employ him to collect some of the money people would owe him. *He* could talk. They used to call him "Callisto." I think it was the name of some famous Spanish politician, a great orator. The people would come to my brother and say, "We will pay you, but please, *please* do not send that man!"

Sept. 29, 1930
Uno, dos, tres, cojita es! Clopin, Clopant, the French say.

There used to be a man in Mayagüez, a beggar, I don't
know how it is now that the Americans have come there,
but in those days they would allow the beggars to come to
the town on Fridays. You would hear one suddenly at the
door: *Alabado sea el nombre de Dios! Hermano—un
limosnita para este pobre.* (Praised be the name of God!
Brother—an alms for this poor creature.) This was one of
those men, very thin without any behind. He would limp.
On Fridays he would come exactly at twelve o'clock when
the boys were getting out of school and they would yell:
La doce es! cola sin punto.

(Two o'clock. Tail but no stop)

. . . . he had written *"mère de glace"*
you know, mother of ice instead of—but you know. And
when the Commandant had corrected him, Perichon had
called him a *palocrin.* This one was furious. You can
imagine, his Commandant!

We were talking about some fish that the boys had
caught—at Oyster Bay. She said: *La ray fa(r)cil l'a mit là!*
What you call it that you put on a tombstone? Epitaph,
that's it! All in notes. Ray is a kind of fish, you know. *La re
fa si la mi la!*

(a stew made of the ray put him there under ground)

Aga Kahn, such an old man to be hurt that way. But,

what good is it to be so old, 102 years they say. You're good for nothing. He is here for seed—as the Spaniards say: *Esta aqui para semillas.* It's silly because it isn't true—but that's what they say. They mean he is all dried up.

Me dice que verseis perlas (quickly after, in good time)
Si vuestro Majestad mas son de cobre
Y como los verse un pobre
Nadie si baja a cojer las.

(This is a famous reply, to the King, made by a poet destined to become famous in the annals of Spain, when he was addressed in the course of an audience. The King had stated addressing the poet directly:

Me dice que verseis perlas (they tell me that you scatter pearls—meaning his words)

The poet replies without hesitation, continuing the given rhyme:

Si vuestro Majestad mas son de cobre

Y como los verse un pobre

Nadie se baja a cojer las

(Yes your majesty, but they are mere copper baubles which since strewn by a poor man no one leans over to pick them up)

June 26, 1930
(Mother—writing the check and forgetting how to write Williams)—like the man who had a fire in his house. He was running around and they asked him where the fire was. He said, I can't remember the name!

Aguanta cachete y caia, porque si viene otra sera peor.

(Take it and shut up, because if you get another, it will be worse)

Well there's one thing I want you to get from this book. It's a Chinese saying: I'll show you. *Poutounkiau, tounby.* Beliefs vary, but reason endures.

When I was a little girl, oh a very little girl, they used to show off with me: I used to dance the Mazurka.

My father and mother must have been like that. Oh, like to tell little stories to make you laugh. My mother used to play the guitar. Madame de Longueville would ask her to play, her name was Adelaïde—A del a ide. And my mother would sing.

A del a ide
li ka fait la belle
li ka fait la belle
li ka fait la belle

in *français patois*—and Mme. de Longueville would laugh and laugh. I don't know why she thought it was so funny.

Miss McEligot would say to me when she was going out —"Now, I'll leave you to your destiny." I didn't know that I talked differently from the others, but she would laugh and say that to me.

Lo que no mata engorde.
(What does not kill, fattens)

Al que Dios no le da hijos, el Diable le da sobriños.

(To him whom God gives no sons, the devil sends cousins)

Neither one thing or the other, grotesques were drawn on the walls of grottos, half human, half leaves—whatever the fancy made obligatory to fate. So in her life, neither one or the other, she stands bridging two cultures, three regions of the world, almost without speech—her life spent in that place completely out of her choice almost, to her, as the Brogbignigans to Gulliver. So gross, so foreign, so dreadful, to her obstinate spirit, that has neither submitted nor mastered, leaving her in a néant of sounds and sense—Only her son, the bridge between herself and a vacancy as of the sky at night, the terrifying emptiness of non-entity.

Mother:

It's a good picture (The Cockeyed World), but it's too common. I don't like the girls to see that. I can't stand it. It makes me . . . Brrrrrr. It makes me feel all shrinking inside. I don't know.

He's going to be a big man—
I like to see a big man, like that. They do things so easily, they pick up those things and put them on their backs as if it was a feather.
I wonder where he gets it.
I had an uncle, my father's brother, who was strong like that. Everybody knew him. They called him "a word and a blow." You know in those times they had no games like

now. He would take a rope and let any three men take
hold of the other end and he would pull them around.

*An exotic little figure. I can see her treading carefully
across the frozen snow she never learned as a child to walk
on balancedly. Pathetic, but resistant—resilient even—
unwilling merely to look on, walking forth anyway,
walking.*

Chagh! she would say, don't eat that.

You know when you wash the rice before you cook it,
sometimes three times, they would save that water. They
used to say it was very good for the skin.
And the water they washed the meat in, a little bloody.
They would use that too, I forget for what.

I have seen my mother take a raw egg, like that, when
it was still warm from the nest. She would open it and
hold it to her eye. They said it was good for that.

I wonder why in French they call these beggars *des
mendiants*. I don't know what it is in Spanish.

Someone is with me today and I don't know who it is.
(Wringing her hands convulsively)
Never mind, you'll find out later.

I would tell him, Some night you will see me, just a
white ghost coming back. He would shiver, No. That's all
right, I won't hurt you. Just coming back to see.

December 22, 1929

(trip to Europe) I don't want to go with any friend. Just put me there on the boat. And no young people. "How are you? How do you feel today?" No. Second class is very good, I don't want to go first class. I can give the woman five dollars and she can take care of me. Only I want to know where I am going, then they can send my things to that place. You say Eliza lives on the *cinquième*. That is supposed to be the best. They always rent the *cinquième* first in France.

That is what I meant when Irving said he believes in fate. What must be will be. (Speaking of Clemenceau) I never wanted to come to America. When my father was dead and my mother died, my brother asked me, Where do you want to go? To America? Nooo! To France? Yesss! I never wanted to come here. Never, never. And yet when I came back from France, I came here. And here I am. I was married here. I have lived here and probably I will die here. And rot here. brrrr. I hate that. I hate it. But don't put me any monument. Put it to your father if you want, but not to me. Let me rot. Brrr. No. I can't think of that.

Memories—old and sweet, the crushing turn, ghosts— associated though with the solid part of her life, children, home, possessions—never realized because of the mirage of the past—
Little left of Martinique, but the stories of the Hibaros —the common people—proverbs: perhaps not Martinique

*at all—more likely Haiti such as, speaking of a small but able man—*Li petit mais caca li gros.

(He's little, but he shits big)

"Practical workers in the army of fate, you and I."

Yes, Mr. Wellcome was the photographer of Puerto Rico and St. Thomas, he went all over taking pictures.

When Pop would come home in the evening tired out, Irving would come downstairs all spic and span. Oh yes, Pop would say, here comes the gentleman. Irving would be all dressed up to kill, shaved and his hair neatly brushed, perfumed and all. But I think the perfume was because of his leg. And not a cent in his pocket.

Your grandmother would always say to them, "Remember, you are a gentleman, your father was one and you are the same."

Poor Godwin, as poor as he was, he would not wear his brother's cast off clothing. No. He wanted his own.

Many people are that way. It is not alone the English. Poor Tinoco. When it would get near to five o'clock he would be all waked up. He would not wait, but he would go into the wash room and begin to clean his hands and fix his hair. Your father called to him one time. I say, Tinoco, the day is not over yet, get to work. You can clean up after five not before. *Pero, Sr. Williams,* replied Tinoco, *Ud. es muy puritano.*

I'll tell you a story, it is true—not very clean, but—one time there were a lot of men at a supper I suppose and they were pulling corks from bottles of beer—or wine, I don't know. Poor Toledo was pulling hard at a cork when a little wind escaped him. Blup! Don Sebastian Sedo quickly turned to him and offered him a cork on the end of a cork screw. That is a true story.

Feb. 6, 1930 (in the hospital)

I can remember a story of my mother-in-law. She would be troubled with gas too. One night she could not stay in bed. So she got up and was walking up and down in the bedroom, up and down. You know in the West Indies the houses are low and the windows were open. She was walking up and down, up and down and making, brummm. Then she would walk a little more and again Brummmm, brrrrup. The man that used to take care of the horses came passing outside, he stopped to listen, "What's that?" he said. "Is that *people*?" She heard, it was dark in the room.

I remember Isobel Paradis de Hibergo—she was my mother's intimate friend. When they changed the money—the machuchner was no good any more—real silver it was all worn out. Sometimes just a little piece of it was left. My mother made a *contra danse* about that. She would sing it and Isobel Paradis wrote it down.

Isobel had a coffee plantation. My mother went there —in the mountains. I never went.

Years afterward when your father was in Spain he went to call on her where she had been living in Madrid. He asked for her and they told him. *Esta de cuerpo presente.* It struck him as very strange, he never forgot it. Her soul had gone, only her body was left. It was very funny that he should go there just at that time. (He is in body here)

I had a letter from Luisa Frasceri, the poor thing with her neck like that! When some people get old they become pessimistic—I don't want to get like that. She speaks about this Roosevelt and all the niggers he is bringing there, male and female. She doesn't say men and women, but male and female. Now we're going to have fun!

You know they are those people who used to be slaves, they don't know anything. Like when they had liberty of cult, you know, all those common people were parading in the street shouting—*Que vive la libertad occulto!* the occult liberty. So ridiculous.

If anybody could have seen me this afternoon, the way I was reading this letter and laughing, they would have thought I was crazy—I sent her two bottles of Florida water—telling her how nice it was and how I knew she would like it. And then this letter thanking me so nicely too for my gift. Then all of a sudden I read—Eso no es Florida, eso es agua de clove this is clove water. And you know, I think she is right, they must be making it cheaper. It is not like it used to be. Perhaps that's what it is.

One day I struck the corner of her tray spilling the milk, orange and coffee.

The old colored servant used to say, "That's all right Missy, anything that can be washed with soap."

On a talkative visitor:
She can talk. It makes me think. In the old times. It
must be different now. But when the *hibaros* would come
into the house you had to be careful because while they
were talking, they would puth! (making the gesture of
spitting) anywhere. So when someone would talk like that,
they would say, *Mi amigo, no espute!* and you knew what
they meant. They didn't even stop to spit.

Many people make a vow. My mother made a vow that if
Carlos should live she would dress him in plain, pure white
until he was two years old. Before that vow, she used to
lose all her children when they were born.

Didn't it rain?
Just a shower.
With *tanto apparato*—I thought it was going to rain all
the evening. (with such a fuss)

Le Corbusier and his new-fangled houses on stilts: it
makes me think of the house where I was born. My mother
had a little place—how you call it—it was not in the city.
I suppose like a little farm. Under it there was nothing. It
had stone steps that went up very easy. It was easy to walk
up them. No, there was nothing under it, just the fresh
air. I remember when I was a little girl I used to like to go
there in my bare feet to get *anuelos* because they would
make me itch and I used to like to scratch them. All that
went to pay Mr. Kruger.

I am awful glad to have found out what is an "arma-

teur." Alice Monsanto told me that my maternal grandfather (a Frenchman) was an "armateur." I just found out
what it means. It means that an "armateur" is a man that
has enough money to equip his own vessel. So he must
have had means.

We never went bathing in the sea. What! take off our
clothes where men could see us! No. Once I remember
I went with my mother, perhaps at five o'clock in the
morning, before anybody was up, to bathe. Then we came
back before anybody could see us. When the Americans
went there and went bathing in their suits with the men,
the people were scandalized, but now that there has
been time for the children to grow up and get used to it—
they are Americans too.

When I first knew your father in Puerto Plata, he lived
in a long low house, what they would call here a bungalow.
It was not more than from here to the street from the sea.
He would go down there and bathe. Your grandmother
would go too sometimes. But there were *baracutas* there.
When the little negro boys would be swimming someone
would watch, then there would be a cry, "Here comes a
baracuta!" and everybody would scramble to get on shore.
Once your father was just going to dive in when he looked
down and saw one quiet in the water looking up at him
and—waiting.

Rosita would say, "Oh Elena, I wish you would marry
Willie."

*Here by the watertank and the stone, mottled granite,
big as a rhinoceros head—cracked on one side—damn
families.*

My grandfather was a business man, you know. He kept
the ice house in Mayagüez. They imported the ice. He
kept it and sold it. My grandmother, my mother's mother,
would make syrups, strawberry and like that. He would sell
them also. But his half brother, Henriquez, there's plenty
of that in my family, would go there, to the ice house, and
drink all day long without paying anything, until the man
my grandfather had there complained. "You know Henriquez comes and drinks five or six glasses of syrup and
never pays anything." He did that. Just drank, lived at the
house, took anything he pleased. That's how, as my mother
says, she came to know Manuel Henriquez, her half cousin,
better than she did her own brother who was away much
of the time studying. Henriquez would never work, help or
do anything until my grandfather had to tell him to stop.
It was at about this time my grandfather died and this is
how my Mother came to distrust and hate the Germans.
All my grandfather's friends were German, all but a few.

It was a man named Krug. I suppose he may have
been father's partner—anyhow, he was his best friend.
I don't know. When my father died Krug came to my
mother and asked her if she had anything because my
father owed him some money. She had a *hacienda*
in the country that she had had since before she was
married, her own. She gave that. Then Krug came
and said it was all gone, that there was nothing left.
After that he turned his back on the family. (The skunk.)
It was the Spanish druggist, Mestre, who lent my mother
the money to buy a few things and sell them to make a

little business. He was a Catalan—they can't say Pepe, like a Castillian but, he would call his wife, Papeeta. My mother would send to Paris for half a dozen fine shirts, but fine, fine shirts and a few things like that. My brother was in Paris studying. When Krug told my mother she must send for him, that there was nothing left, she wrote. He answered her that he would sweep the streets of Paris rather than leave. She would send him money she made on her little business. Sometimes, he told us afterward, he would keep a *sou* in his pocket two weeks so as not to say he hadn't any money. The students helped each other. Barclay, an Englishman, was one of his best friends. He helped him.

*That's why my own mother's education ended abruptly. Some times she would copy out letters for my grand-mother, child that she was, to send to Paris. When her brother returned a doctor, he himself sent her to Paris to study painting. But he married and he began to have children and he never collected any money—he had a wife too. So finally he sent for my mother to go back to Santo Domingo where they were living then. Mother cried for three days; then she had to go and leave it all. When she got there, her brother told her about his friend, . . . A fine fellow, the best in the world "pero no es musico".
. . . was in the States at the time of my mother's return from Paris having his teeth fixed.*

When a little child would be bothersome, they would tell her to go ask the maid for a little piece of *ten te aya*. (get out of here)

When my brother was happy, he would sing, walking up and down kicking out his feet: *Si j'étais roi de Bayaussi— et tu serais reine—et par ma foi.* You made me think of him right away. (If I were King of Bayaussi—you should be my Queen—believe me)

I remember we had little silver plaques with a chain on it to hang over the necks of the bottles, whisky, brandy or whatever it was. And a box of some kind of wood, not for the kitchen, but a pretty box. Inside it was lined with something like yes, pewter, all inside, and there was a cover of metal too with a little knob on it, all inside the wooden box. You would open the outer cover and inside was the lid. When you would take that off, you would see the tea with a silver spoon for taking it out.

But now, here are the roses, three opening. Out of love. For she loves them and so they are there. They are not a picture. Holbein never saw pink thorns in such a light. Nor did Massachio. The petals are delicate, it is a question if they will open at all and not drop, loosing at one edge and falling tomorrow all in a heap. All around the roses there is today, machinery leaning upon the stem, an aeroplane is upon one leaf where a worm lies curled. Happy it seems and enormous, it seems to hold up the sky for it has no size at all. We eat beside it—beside the three roses that she loves. And an oak tree grows out of my shoulders. Its roots are my arms and my legs. The air is a field. Yellow and red grass are writing their signatures everywhere.

They never know when to stop, even the wonderful
Patti. Your father was crazy about her. I wonder if anybody went so high. She would go way up, up, up. You
wondered when she was going to stop. I wonder which is
worst to be young or old. You cannot get what you want.
Oh my goodness, old! Your knees are stiff, your fingers
are crooked, your voice is gone, your memory is going. You
want to do, but you can't. That is why artists make a fool
of themselves. They never know when to stop. They *think*
they can, but they can't.

Well, what's the news?

*It's still positive. I'm sorry but—it's the truth. I wish
I could help you.*

It's terrible.

—there are no rivers. I remember one winter all the
water was frozen. The only place we could get water was at
Demarest's, he had a cistern in the yard.

I wonder how they do now. They had nothing, but well
water. They had big cisterns. Where else could they get
it?

*I like Chopin because he was honest and good and he
was a genius and he could play the profound, and tremen-
dous states of being cannot exist here—that is the ultimate
felicities of understanding, we rise to our occasions like
starved trout to a flake of tobacco leaf, therefore, our
staccato verse and fragmentary prose. To stay on a point
or a plane is huge work not possible when one is in-
evitably opposed by many, the one must go down the*

scale to succeed or be content to touch understanding only by flashes. Mammie look at the little flowers they are growing. The greater swallows the rest: If my legs were tougher I'd play baseball tomorrow which proves that muscles are of no importance, but that weakness is excessively to the point. He did not know it, but he was born to be smothered in ammonia. I'll bend the God damned parallels until they meet O elm before their bedroom windows blossoming.

El desprecio es el mejor castigo—
(Scorn is the best punishment)

After another had ben talking for a long time excitedly. um HUM! *Jene vous dis pas non* (I don't say no to you)

To tell you the truth I could have stayed there (in France), but I was afraid of the father of those two girls—fooling around. I was afraid of him.

Le doy un gateso a cualquiere Isabel Paradiso de Hiberga.
(I'd give a slap in the face to someone)

As Papa used to say, "Why don't you make a list, Monday this, Tuesday that, and so on, for the week." No, I couldn't do that. Perhaps it is a fault, I am too restless. In fact all my life I have reproached myself that I haven't a *parti pris.* The same in cooking.

Sometimes they would send a girl into the country—

on business and she would not return. The negroes would catch them and eat them—so they would believe.

Thank God for modern poetry, for poetry—alive that is. It is the only thing that gives any satisfaction, the only thing in the world worth living for (a painter might say the same about painting)—and Ezra Pound, thank God, is doing his part.

Well, either he had to burst or go ahead because that's the only thing he's doing.

Jan. 4, 1928

I can remember—that makes me think of it—how the boys would go in the streets selling ice cream, with the freezer carried on their shoulders—*Elado de mantechado, elado de pina. En la variation esta el gusto!* That's what they would say. That is why I do not like to think of going back. All those things would be lost.

Make haste!—I can't make "make haste" M'am. That's St. Thomas.

I'm awful sorry for those doctors—some of them are young. Not so much for Nobile, it's his own fault. It's a shame, three of them drifting on a piece of ice God knows where. What do they want to go there for, nobody's going to plant potatoes over there.

O'Rourch, you know, that used to work for me, he had a funny idea. All the flowers that used to be growing over there he used to call them alfalfa. Haha. What shall I do with all that alfalfa? he used to say.

I suppose I was so romantic when I was a child—that's why. I remember my mother had a friend Maria Louisa Blum. A little colored boy would come with the milk in the morning and always with a bunch of flowers, all with the dew on them. It's so pretty, it feels pretty to see them.

We must have been very young. We would go to the river to bathe, early in the morning. There we would jump around in the water naked. I remember there were yucca leaves, big leaves growing in the water. When you would throw water up on them, it would run down all silver.

Once—you know after they cut the sugar cane they leave the small canes that are too little to cut. Some of the children said, "Let us go in and get some." When they were in there, they yelled, "Here comes the Major Domo." I tell you I ran. He was on a horse. Just when I was home, he rode up to me and said, "Well, you *can* run." I shall never forget it.

I can remember, on New Year's day, in Puerto Rico, the colored people would come into the town from the estates —from all parts of Africa I suppose they were—and they would dance. I remember one who had a kind of hoop, I suppose, around him and palm leaves hanging like a kind of skirt,—dancing his wild dance, jumping and shouting. There was another, a silly looking fellow in a long shirt to his knees, who went shuffling along looking over his shoulder with a sly grin; then when he would see many women together he would flip up his shirt front at them and snap it down again and shuffle away sidelong with a ridiculous leer.

> *Con la sal que derrama una morena*
> *Se mantiene una rubia semana y media*
> (With the salt you'd take for a brunette
> You'd keep a red head a week and a half)

When I think of it—the best days are gone for nothing. I mean to say and the worst days are coming.

I knew a Spanish officer with *grado de commandante* who had a long, long neck.

Clavel de Muertos! What do you call them? Marigolds. In Puerto Rico they grow easily in the country so they have them for the dead people.

Papa liked his corn old; he always picked out the older looking pieces—tai-tai, as they say in Puerto Rico.

Put it in your little bem-bem!

When my father was small, they were very poor. He said for amusement they would sometimes hire an old horse and take turns riding it. But they would not wait for the other to come back to the starting point, but they would run beside the horse all the way there and back. I don't know whether his stepfather was there then—that is why there were so many in the family. He was Hoheb, but his half brothers and sisters were Henriquez. He was the only one that stuck to his mother and her sister, I think. Once he ran away and hid in a ship to come to America, but they caught him and he had to go back.

Mme. de Joinville had a boarding school in Mayagüez. Her daughter married again. Mrs. Green—she only thinks of her house. It is full of china and furniture. She will have a cushion with a head of a woman on it—you know how they are and perhaps she will embroider a string of beads around the woman's neck. Very bad taste!

Yes, she won the lottery of life.

When he was a little boy he would be left with the other children in the house, he could not have been much older than they, while she went to practice with the Episcopal Church choir. He would wait for the eight o'clock cannon to be fired. He would be so frightened that he would hide his head under the pillow as eight o'clock came near. She used to be a flirt Mrs. Todd said, she would go horseback riding with the Episcopal minister.

I was playing the piano in the parlor and Godwin was sitting in the dining room. All of a sudden he ran into the room, "Ugh!" he said, and stood there trembling.

"What is it, Godwin?" I said. But he said something had come and frightened him. At night he would come and knock on my door, but I would not open it. I could hear him walking up and down in the attic all night long. He didn't like the smell of the moth balls I put in the closets there. He said it was like hell. It frightened him. I remember how he looked at Mrs. Dodd. She didn't know it, but such a smile on his face as he was leaning on the door as much as to say, wait a little bit. He wanted to kill her. He thought she was making the evil spirits come for him.

Once Grandma came all out of breath to tell us that three loud knocks had answered her when she asked if it was a spirit. I wonder if he did not do it.

Yes, and I remember a family in Puerto Rico: he died of tuberculosis; then she died of it and a daughter died of tuberculosis, and a son died of tuberculosis, and the older son, his mother used to say, because I used to play with them, when these two grow up they will marry, well he died of tuberculosis and Pepe died of tuberculosis and I remember one of the girls, she was married already, one day she was eating *guava* paste and that cheese, what do you call it? Cottage cheese, when bruuup! She vomited pure blood, they were all laughing and eating around in a little circle when she vomited pure blood. Pepe came to New York and what do you think? An American Insurance Company insured him! Now THAT was a cheat because you could see he had tuberculosis when you saw him.

Adelaide de Joinville, she had so many children, that is why when her husband died, although she was of the *haut monde* she had to open a school—all of her children did something. And there was a Mrs. Minot, she would dress good, it was expensive, but she looked awful. She used to go like a duck, like this! I remember one day we were on a balcony. Goodness how we laughed! Mrs. Minot was passing and Mme. de Joinville was saluting her: *Bonjour, ma chérie!* Then she would turn to us and whisper, *Mon dieu, quelle dégene! Adieu, ma belle enfant. Dieu quelle—!*

(My God, what a fright! Adieu, my pretty child! God what—etc.)

What killed her was—she had a daughter married to Mr. Schaumloeffel. He was a good friend, but he had one of these hard heads, hard, hard, hard. He forced his little daughter to eat a certain kind of cereal. She did not like it, but he would not let her have anything else. She got weaker and weaker. They called the doctor. At that time the baby was given to a nurse—a fat little thing, like that! Patapouff! Well, while they were watching the girl, the baby was taken sick and in two weeks they buried them both. Mme. de Joinville cried and cried and cried,—she felt worse than the parents. They never had any more children and I think it was that that killed her.

Mr. Schaumloeffel was a good friend, but he was one of those *bons viveurs*—he had a big house.

I feel glad he didn't suffer. I said in his ear, I am going to call Willie, and when you came he smiled. Only once in a while he asked for an *Antikamnia* tablet, and not very often. Do you think he had a cerebral hemorrhage?

I think they should have done an autopsy. He made a motion like that, with his hands as if to say, I am going. No, I believe there is a soul, something that lives. I know when I talk about a person that is dead I feel something inside me, as if something wants to break. Mr. Monet used to say there were spirits that were interested in their family and their homes, they were earthbound and did not dare to go to the heights. These were the ones that could be called back. But the high ones never returned, or only to very spiritual people. He believed in Job and many others. But Mrs. Higginbottom who belonged to the United Brethren called me aside one day when she knew that we were interested in Spiritualism and said to me, "Don't let Mrs. Walcott lead you astray. Don't let her talk to you about the spirits. Only the bad spirits come back to the earth."—She liked me and wanted to save my soul and she thought Grandma was a bad influence. It was she who one evening put a piece of the hair of one of Jimmy Hazel's brothers who was crazy into my hand to see what would happen. I went completely out of my head. Papa was frightened I can tell you. He would not even let me talk or open my mouth after that. Once at Mr. Borschneck's house Mr. Demarest was talking to a spirit. Everybody was silent and he asked who it was when all of a sudden the clock said, Coo-coo! Mrs. Mathews laughed so hard she couldn't stop. Everybody laughed.

The theosophists think that the personality does not exist—but not the spiritualists.

Good gracious, I can't remember their names: Mme. Givry. She was a little old woman, very talkative, as you know. One day when she had finished eating, she took her glass of water and poured it over her fingers into her tea cup. It was empty you know, but it made such a funny impression on me. Her daughter, I can't think of her name. She was very tall. They said she was in love with Ludovic, she was married you know, but she liked him very much. Then there was a man, what was his name? They were afraid to invite him because he liked to shock the people. He would say anything that came into his mind. He liked it. He would come with all his decorations on his chest. *"Je viens avec toute ma ferblanterie,"* he would say. They say he was full of wounds all over. He would say, I have so many holes all through me *"sans counter le trou de mon cul."* Then everyone would hide his face or look away.

Mme. de Tourneville they said had been a very handsome woman. Her cousin had fallen in love with her when he was still a boy. You know sometimes a young boy will fall in love with an older woman that way when she is handsome. He was her cousin. They sent him to Africa, but he came back and married her. She was twenty years older than he. But she was still handsome. He used to like to dance with me. Alice used to say, "You mustn't dance too much with that man, his wife is very jealous of him you know."—He was very straight, a military man, and his face was dark from sunburn. My cousin when he would introduce me, they always want to make an impression, he couldn't think of anything else to say so he told them:

"This is the sister of the greatest doctor in Puerto Rico."
You know. There was also the Baroness d'Ortesse—there
was nothing to tell that she was different from anybody
else. I wish I could remember more of their names. There
was another woman very tall who had a squint eye, like
that.

She's like Santo Thomas as the Catholics say—she likes
to put her finger in the wound—to be sure it's there.

If you had known Mrs. Adams, she could have told you
everything that I was. Poor soul, she was the last of the
de Longuevilles. She was a good friend. When the girls
would come, I would make my lip very dry and fold it up
and lie on the bed and roll my eyes up—and scare the life
out of them.

In the French school where I went when I was a little
girl, there was an old servant, Avriette. She was so old
that when she would lean over some wind would come out
and she would make a noise, brrrrrrrp! So we would make
fun of her: *Avriette! tirez nous petez BOOM! le navire est
arrivé!*
(Avriette! Fire us BOOM! the ship has come to port!)
Now don't you go put that into your book—or I won't
tell you *any*thing.

One of our amusements—it makes me ashamed. You
know there are little lizards down there. The boys would
kill them sometimes. Oh about *that* long, as long as your

hand. There were three or four of us little girls, and one little darkie, her name was Celestine. We had a little burying ground and we would take the little lizards the boys killed and bury them. It was great fun. We would have a funeral and fix a grave with flowers, very pretty. Charlot would love funerals. Down there they would—in that time—fix the little children that died all with flowers, all round it. Charlot would jump up and down and clap his hands when he would see them coming. Here comes a funeral! and he would run out to the gate to see.

Ten miles deep inside its sleeping form a little boy whom later she would fit into her hollowness, her son— preordained by chance—free to run, now that it was April, ran. His legs seemed to bounce by themselves under him, he scarcely knew how they could go so fast—or that they were legs—He desired and, riding his pleasure, he arrived and took.

It was all in a great yard with a painted wooden fence of boards, cut out into a scroll design and painted green and red—that stood above his head—but he could peek through and see the people passing.

Behind him his smaller brother, six years old or less, came following while the mother leaned upon the balustrade of the balcony that encircled the house and watched them play.

There above them, as they played, leaned nothing of America, but Puerto Rico, a foreign island in a tropical sea of earlier years—and Paris of the later Seventies.

Oct. 18, 1936

I had another dream last night: I was in a big park and I wanted to find the center of it—the exact center—I don't know why. And I was walking. There were a lot of people and big iron sticks to tell you where to go. Then I saw a few people standing and I went to them and it was Mr. and Mrs. Rhodes. I explained to them that I wanted to get a necklace to give to you (to Florence). And Mrs. Rhodes said, "That's all right, I'll get you one from my maid. She has plenty of them." So the maid brought me a necklace. I wanted to pay for it, but Mrs. Rhodes said, "No, never mind, she has plenty of them, you keep it." So I kept it and gave it to you. Wasn't that a funny dream? I wonder what they mean, dreams like that.

I could eat all those grapes, I said.
You couldn't!
Yes, as full as I am I could eat every one of them.
I say, I could eat all of those grapes.
They are so pretty you eat them first with your eyes.

There's no way to tell anyone anything. If Floss takes my mother three fall violets that have bloomed because of the warm weather, my mother will say, with a gloomy face: I wish I had stayed at the shore so as not to make so much trouble for you—and Floss very justly wants to throw the flowers in her face.

pleu per voi que per me—
(Weep for you as for me)

(cemetery) Is this where they bury the Rutherford people?

(picture) Yes, just the way she looked. I'm glad I did one. I wish I had done more like that before I was married. I can remember that little collar. Gracious! didn't I feel bad when I had to come back.

Hace mucho neblito
(The clouds are hanging low)

They sent me a poem from the church once. I read it, but it was so stupid I never read any again. They send them very often.

I think those little tablets you gave me have relieved the pain in the knees. I don't know whether it's that or *por casualidad.* (by accident)

In bare feet and pajamas I stopped on the way to the bath room one morning hearing what seemed to be incoherent talking in her room—I thought she might be trying to call me. It made no sense and frightened me: Es. Es. Esta. Es. Esta. Esta. Es. Es. I was afraid to go into the room not knowing what I might find.

When I went, after a moment of listening, walking quietly, I put my head forward past the door not wishing to disturb her, there I saw her sitting up in bed, propped against the pillows quite comfortably and saying as before: Es. Esta. Es. Es. Es. Esta.

I went in. She looked up and smiled. I'm all right, she said.

*Good, I answered and went out. I didn't want her to
know what I had been thinking. I presumed that she had
not been satisfied with the way she had been pronouncing
the S sound—with false teeth and little talking—so she
had decided to practice it in an idle moment while waiting for me to bring her her breakfast.*

I didn't go to any *porranda*. But I went to sleep at half
past two. So I was shaky this morning.

There is a kind of orange in Puerto Rico that I have
never seen here. I don't think they send it away. It is
half orange, half grapefruit, sort of bitter sweet. The
natives say that if you drink the juice of it and then take
a cup of coffee it is good for the fever. It has a rough kind
of skin, like big pores. They call it *torongha*.

And there is another orange, like an orange only much
smaller and it is always green. Green, green, green. It
never gets yellow. The taste is just sugar and water, no
taste at all, but very sweet. Or perhaps just the least taste
of orange. They call it *lima*. The same as Lima in South
America.

My aunt in St. Thomas, she had the reputation for
making good cake. But she used lots of eggs and butter.

I remember once I said—Mr. Badger was looking at me:
Santa Torpesa! *ora pro nobis!* He looked at me so funny.
He was surprised. Saint Stupidity, pray for us.

Alfredo was so stupid, he could have been a dentist now with an office of his own. But he wouldn't study. He made a fool of himself.

When my brother received his *baccalauréat*—he wrote a letter. I can still see it, in big letters: *VICTOIRE!* I tell you he went through a hard time too. I can see my mother praying and praying and praying, that he would succeed. She worked hard to keep him there.

Wherever you go you see those Italians digging up things in the fields. Well, they are used to be poor.

I feel like reading—and I don't feel like reading. Everything is like a veil before me. I'm getting blind.

Yes, she married a man called *le Merdet!*

—like you remember the name. They were two partners and one was called Vachier—Mr. Vachier and the other Lavalle—*M. Vachier et M. Lavalle.*

What are you looking for?
A screw driver. Have you got one in the sewing machine?
No, but I have something to punch a hole. But don't you lose it?

Can you see with that light?
Much, yes! with a bow.

It's remarkable—what she can do, and what a digestion!

When you are learning a language many funny things happen. I can remember how it impressed me when Julie Monsanto said, "What a cheek!" I thought that was awful funny. I can still see her. What a cheek! And they would say "boids". At first I didn't know what they were saying. Then I found out it was "birds". I thought that was the way to say it because in St. Thomas they would say "bierrrds".

I suppose now it is different with the schools, but in the old days the common people used to speak very badly. They never said "para", you know, for. They always said "pa' ". So when Meg came from there and asked me the names of the children and I told her "Palamona" she said, Don't let her go there—*"Pa' la monja"*.—It means "for the monkey".

I knew a colored man who wanted to speak Spanish well so he put an "s" on every word!

You see that shade there (my shadow on the wall with the light behind us coming upstairs) well, that's the way I see with this eye, the right eye.

I knew a black man, he was a shoemaker and he burst his one eye with a needle, pulling it. You never can tell about such things.

The weeping willow and Alfred de Musset, he wanted it on his tomb.

Mariquita—they throw money at every christening,

sometimes even gold. Everybody has a piece of money. When I was christened I had a band around my waist full of gold pieces.

She had written "Orien": I know very well to put "Orient"—but I'm stupid nowadays.

Poor man he used to say, the English is a funny language. You say chicken and then you say kitchen and I never know which it is.

My Uncle Manuel, big fat fellow, red face. Every morning he took his coffee with an egg beaten in it. You know how you beat an egg with sugar—you boys used to like it that way. Then he would pour his coffee in there. Very rich.

Mon cher enfant si tu te sens toujours malade, it faut demander à Mme. Brunel de te laisser venir chez moi pour que je te donne quelque médicament à prendre.

J'espère tout de même que tu vas mieux aujourd'hui. Sois prudent.

Ta mère qui t'aime.

(My dear child: If you still feel sick, ask Mrs. Brunel to let you come to me so that I can give you some medicine. I hope, in spite of that, you feel better today. Take care of yourself. Your mother who loves you.)

(A little job for a Boy Scout)
"There is always room for an honest person"—

The one who would bring back our little dog will be

rewarded by Dr. W. C. Williams.
We have reared the little animal from a little puppy and he forms a part of the family.

There was a man here that lost his voice like that. He thought he'd never speak again. But it came back overnight.
He woke up one morning and it came back out loud. Near scared him to death he'd been silent so long you know.

(Her only poem!)

—Por mi ventana—	From My Window
Mira mira como vuelan!	Look, look how they fall
Son las hojas destacadas	They are the dried leaves
del inexorable Otono.	of the inexorable Autumn
No hay porque aflijirse	No need to be sorrowful
ellas volveran	they will relive
en la radiante Primavera,	in the radiant Springtime
Ay! de mi, las ilusiones perdidas	Alas, for lost illusions
son hojas caidas del arbol del corazon	they are leaves falling from the tree of the heart
esas no volveran,	these will not relive
Muertas estan en el Ibierno de la vida humana.	But they are dead in the Winter of human life.

Sometimes I have such funny dreams I have to laugh myself. It was not tonight, but last night. Mr. Luce gave me one of those disjointed dolls to hold in my arms. I thought I was going to hear of someone dead today or something.

One day (at the shore) it was so cold the butter was hard, hard. You couldn't put a knife in it. (Showing how you could poke the butter without effect.) It could roll on the floor without making a mess.

Look Nana, said Floss, showing her a flower in a little white jar. Isn't it pretty? What kind of flower is that? *They call it an African violet. They are like our violets, but they have no odor.* Oh, isn't that pretty, said my mother, Let me see. So pretty.—*I could see her drawing it closer—Finally she leaned her head close to it: She smelled it and said,* That's true, not the faintest—

I suppose they are killing each other in Spain as usual. It seems a pity that they should destroy those beautiful buildings—for what? It makes me feel irritated. But if it had been France I would be heartbroken. So now I know how I feel. I know which one I love.

Of course, my pains are worse. What I felt in my hip I feel now also in my shoulder. But I suppose there is nothing to do. This medicine is not for me. You can take it. It says it is for when the urine is "green"; my urine isn't green. This must be for something else.

Caracoles! that hurts! (Trimming her corns.) The chiropodists have something they put on it—to soften it.

My leg was pretty bad today. But I insist, I walk any-way—I was headstrong.

If you have something to do in Passaic you could take me there and when you are through with what you are doing you can pick me up on the way back.

I do' know. She just said she didn't feel well and she lay down and she died. Yes, she was a Christianscience.

He's getting a boil on his leg. I don't think he is well. I hate to see him with that cat fever. He's always rubbing his eyes and his nose (with appropriate gesture), it makes me feel uncomfortable to see him.

The fish man brought me some fish. It smelled strong. It wasn't rotten, but it didn't smell good. I told him to take the paper it was in and take it far away. He came the next week with a little piece of fish for me. He said he wanted me to have a little fish before I went home. But I told him no! no! I didn't want it. It made me sick to my stomach even to smell it.

What kind of apple is this? It tastes good, it has a special kind of taste. A what? A MacIntosh. Very good. It makes me think of Kai. He enjoyed apples so much.

We have to go to a wedding tonight.
Who is getting married?
One of Mrs. D's daughters.

And who is the happy fellow?
Someone from New York. I don't know.

At the top of the stairs one day, today, in time with
her cane and her limping step she began to recite—
      Crinoline from back to back
      It's a new fashion come in—
It's a song the negroes of St. Thomas used to sing. You can
imagine at what time that was. They made a song for
everything—I noticed a peculiar halt in the second line
through the word "fashion", a drag in the pace which is
a sign of the "contradance" of the locality.

We were eating grapes, large red California grapes
which I was cutting from a large bunch. She wondered
what the vine must have been like to bear such heavy
bunches. In St. Thomas, she began during a pause in the
conversation, my godmother, Mrs. Pardon, used to have
a grape vine in her yard. It was all fixed up beautifully.
There were not many leaves, but here and there would
be a bunch of grapes, but each one was in a paper bag—
for the birds, I suppose, or for some other reason.

Did you ever live in St. Thomas?

No, but I used to go there with my mother. Wherever
she went I had to go, there was nobody to leave me with
I suppose. We would stay about fifteen days with her
friend, Mrs. Pardo. She would buy things there, a few
shorts, a coat and other things to sell again in Puerto

Rico. Now that I think of it she must have been a clever woman, a good business woman.

How did you go there, in a sail boat?

No—with indignation—in a STEAMer—with a wheel on the outside.—An appropriate gesture with the right hand and arm, turning.

How long did it take up?

Let me try to remember, I think eight days. Eight days! Yes, about eight days. Now, I suppose they go in a few hours. *Se le pego las sabanas.*

(The sheets stuck to him—meaning he didn't want to get up).

If we were bitten by a bee or anything, they used to run and get three different kinds of leaves—any leaves so long as they were three different kinds to rub on.

I'll sit here for five minutes so as not to say, *Adios Blas, ya comiste, ya te vas.* (Good bye, Blas, now you've eaten, now you leave.)

A red rose in the garden: It seems to me that is the smell of the roses in that circle there in France—the first summer that I went.

I don't know. I don't want to think of it. I couldn't understand why they were writing to me—I was already dead. I couldn't understand it. I thought I was going crazy.

Her legs (Cousin Anita) were so fat she didn't wear any

drawers—her legs came so close together. But she wore *pantalettes,* just from her knees to the ankles, so no one could see them.

Anita would laugh because my mother used to look at her legs and ask her if they were swollen—they were so big.

At Mayagüez, oh many years ago! they would come at eight o'clock in the morning and yell, *Pan de la machina, caliente! Pan de la machina, caliente!* hot bread for breakfast. (Bread fresh from the oven! Bread out of the oven, piping hot!).

And you would see a chicken hanging on the bush. The papaya. It's like a bush or a little tree. Not very long. But they would hang it there to get tender.

Come on now, I'll give you a ride in the country— Rutherford style, and I turned the car off the main highway into a few hundred feet remaining on an old dirt road along the river.

This reminds me of the roads in the West Indies in the olden time. There was so much dust we had to sweep the houses in the morning and in the afternoon—with the windows open the way the people lived.

Aren't those grasses pretty.

She hesitated. I only see a kind of smooth thing, kind of pinkish.

I always thought whatever country you were born in,

that's what you were. If you were born in France you were a Frenchman, if you were born in Germany you were a German and like that. But I remember once, I think it was a peddler and I asked him what nationality he was and he said a Jew. I was so surprised. I thought it didn't make any difference what religion you were or from what country. Anyhow, they are sincere. They don't care what the universe may say, they are a Jew, that's all, it settles it.

I haven't got rid of my infancy. I like ribbons, I like little things like that (an ash receiver in the shape of a little warming pan).

Thank you son, I'm just here like a—*crab!*
We have nothing, but beans today.
Le piano des pauvres. (Poor man's piano)

Are they wealthy those DuPonts? They sound French, are they French?
I replied that they were. She answered:
The President's son *se puse las botas!* (he wants to get on).

What is that? (poking her left index finger into the sugared top) Hot cross bun? *Cold* hot cross bun (with a smile) I realized she had felt it to determine its temperature.

Easter Sunday (1937): This morning we're going to St. Patrick's Cathedral to see it. Ah! oh yes! Great doings!

People go away and you never see them again. There was a little girl who was my intimate friend when we were in school. She was blond and I was brunette. Celestine Cavaliere. She had no mother and my mother used to dress her and sew for her sometimes. She went and I never heard from her to this day.

A childlike innocence, unaffected by age with its maddening mutilations—remains still her virtue. To some it is childish, all the characteristics of a spoiled child—which she was—with her bad temper, fears, vindictiveness of an undisciplined infant. To others an indestructibleness, a permanence in defiance of the offensive discipline which is only a virtue to those who wish to flatten out every rebellious instinct down to a highway levelness for their own crazy facility. Be that as it may she has not given in. And is still, as a child, amused.

That's a kiss with a whip! she said this morning when as I kissed her the handles from the ropes she used to lift herself in bed struck her on the left cheek. And she smiled.

I met the tailor coming downstairs. I wondered who it was as I had come in from the back and supposed the house empty. We are good friends. He looked at me and smiled, shaking his head. She wants a dress with long sleeves, he said. There isn't a dress like that in the whole of New York for sale today.

The great variety of the world—the tropic fruit—Fruitful—the flowers, Renoir; variety important because it allows mutation, the aspects of a life—from enough view-

points to ascertain more accurately the truth and the character of the good.

She never went back to her native land, neither one of them did for that matter. It was only a short ship's journey and dozens of the others came to our house in the course of thirty years and were returned—while Pop at least sailed all around the place, to Central America, everywhere. But she never did more than go to Paris and Geneva with us boys. I don't think she ever thought of going. Then after the Spanish-American War she flatly refused, bitterly, in fact.

The Monsantos, Enriqueses, and Hohebs are all mixed up in the telling about them. Apparently they came from Amsterdam—she remembers portraits in Dutch costume, but cousin Sissy hated old things and they all were destroyed finally. Hoheb, the father, was of a first marriage and the half brothers Enriquez, were always in his hair. How many generations there had been in Mayagüez and how they had mixed with the Spanish, is completely lost.

The May Auto Ride—returning:

You remember the track where Godwin used to go to the races? Well, it used to be here.

Yes, some men are very much interested in horses. Your Uncle Irving was like that. He didn't have, as the Spanish say, *ni donde caer morte* (nor a place to die), but I suppose any little money he could get he would enjoy betting. He never won anything.

That old tree looks like an animal.

Nothing is known of our family beyond the last three generations and not all of that—other than vague rumors, enticing, irritating, scandalous—racially doubtful in certain cases. But there was vigor there and sensibility, even intelligence—on both sides.

We are of those who came to the United States through the West Indies. On one side, the maternal, no one knows how long ago the originals had gone there, but on the other no earlier than in the 1850's. The later move by William George Williams and his wife *née* Raquel Elaine Rose Hoheb came years later. We are the first to have been born here.

I wish the carpenters would get through.
Well, they never hurry.
No, they are very good workers—and very neat.
I always thought it would be very nice, carpentry—or masonry.
I should prefer carpentry.
Well, masonry. To take a little plaster and put the stones together.

This rose makes me think. It must have been at Cavour, where we went some times in the summer. There was a rose like that growing in the middle of the garden. It had the same smell. Very sweet.

Jack Lucy was here. But he didn't want to come in.
He didn't want to come in? *Imbecile!* let him go.

What you call those birds? Not sparrow. Like Albert
has. Parrot. That's it. You say to them *povite, povite* and
they put down the head for you to scratch it.

What a trouble in the world.—*We had been discussing
in the usual passionate way the arrival of a Teutonic archi-
tect—whom my brother had been initiating into the
mysteries of American ways:* We order what material we
need and in six months perhaps we get it—perhaps not. In
this country, mother said we telephone for our material
and they send it the same day. He couldn't believe it.
Hitler, naturally, was up at the breakfast table. He's a
DESPOT! Why certainly, like all despots since Babylon.
Desperate needs breed desperate measures for their cure.
*But she had been delighted to find a GERMAN who
wanted to become an American citizen and who had said,
Der Führer! with a smile and a sneer.*

Then I aimed and fired! *Anyhow, the Prince of Wales
is happy.*

Humph! perhaps so—with that woman. *She will be a
good wife for him. After all, he isn't a child.*

Maybe externally he will be happy—He may be happy
on the outside, but *la procession anda por dentro! dicen
por aya.*

I will speak of when I was a little girl—*en el tiempo,*
many years ago. That reminds me. We had a little colored

boy who was sick. I don't know what was the matter, diarrhea—something like that—I don't know what. My mother called Dr. Block and he told them not to give him anything to eat. So they kept him there in bed. But at night he got up and went to the kitchen. He found one of those Dutch cheeses, you know. It was very hard, but he ate the whole thing. And it cured him. He wasn't sick after that time. It didn't do him any harm. On the contrary.

I asked Sonny how he liked his work in the hospital. He said, Too much study. My Mother was like that, she never gossiped, she never said much. She was very quiet and never spoke loud. My brother was the same.

Paris: I was there three years, a little more than that. We lived on the Rue Notre Dame des Champs—near the Luxembourg. It was close to the rue de Seine where I would go to the *Institut.* I lived with Alice and Ludovic. It was an apartment, on the ninth floor. Mme. Farine lived close by on the Boulevard St. Michel. They were all poor. What money will do to a person in this life! If Alice had not been so mean perhaps I would have stayed there longer.

Having told her about the book and possible success— I am thrilled. I hope it is a success. But then I feel afraid. I wish I wasn't like that, but I have been that way all my life. It spoils everything. If you have money, then you can feel secure. If you can say I want to do a thing and you do it, that's why people want money.

Sometimes I sit thinking of anything—all sorts of things come into my head. There were two old men, very old and half asleep that were talking together and one of them said to the other—

    Pues, yo ya.   (Well, here am I)

and the other answers him—

    Pues, ya yo.   (Well, I am here)

From there he went to Mayagüez in partnership with Langmeyer and Krug. They were, I suppose, what you call merchants. They would buy the whole cargo of a ship coming from Europe and sell it.

I only knew your father ten months before I married him. It was in Puerto Plata. My brother was there so when I came back from France that is where I went. You could see the Wellcome House from where we lived.

My father died when I was eight years old.

Your father came to our house every night when I was there, so much so that his mother sent his trunk one night and told him to stay. He came to New York to have his teeth fixed. Then I came too and we were married here— in Jersey City—at Mrs. Monsanto.

My mother must have been very nervous. If you only showed her a pistol she thought she was already shot. She couldn't bear to have you whisper to her, she said it tickled her so she could not stand it. She died when I was fifteen or sixteen. My brother wanted to send me away. He asked me if I wanted to go to the United States or to France. I told him, France! To Paris!

In the West Indies, in St. Thomas, Puerto Rico, Santo

*Domingo—the races of the world mingled and intermar-
ried—imparting their traits one to another and forgetting
the orthodoxy of their ancient and medieval view. It is a
trait of the tradition of learning and of the attempt of the
race of man to find security in the world to adore the old.
The best of it is believed caught and held—so we all talk
and even believe, in spite of ourselves in the old as of great
value—even superlative beyond our grasp—the classic.*

*In this classic we forget that all the rigidities of evil lie
embedded which the radical, the dreaded radical of the
world would destroy. In the West Indies of the middle of
the nineteenth century, in those small towns great changes
were taking place. Not all was good though. Many rigidities
were perpetuated, many stupidities of classic proportions
were entrenched.*

*Yet the races mingled with man and woman sensing the
new in superb disregard for a tradition which, indeed, they
had left behind, simply didn't know any more. The girl
admired Sol Hoheb and—I suppose they learned each
others languages fast enough.*

*Great gold came from these things, greater than the
metal they killed the natives for and drove them to death
by group suicide to circumvent. The devil of conformity
which peopled them under Torquemada wasn't allowed to
sleep entirely in New Spain. Evil opposed good. The line is
sharply drawn as it is in the character of my mother.*

*This is important, and important not to confuse, since it
casts the only illumination today in a world slipping toward evil by economic chains—as it slipped through the
persecution, the St. Bartholomews Eve, the Cromwellian*

*murders in Ireland—in all other parts of the world—as it
flares again today—sadly mixed—but easy to differentiate
by the model of the West Indies of those days in modern
politics.*

*The authorities are always backward, England protect-
ing its possessions, Russia—thus to understand, as an example the fascist tendency, as exemplified by the German
Nazi—in the light of the old West Indian teaching and
life—Talmudic in character. An old Jewish woman whose
ancestors had lived continuously in Berlin for two hundred
and fifty years, ill, distinguished, is expelled by official de-
cree. This would be abhorrent to that viewpoint.*

*But, in the light of the same teaching, it is wise to pause
and reexamine the conditions. It is precisely the racial
solidarity, the traditional aloofness of the nomadic tribe,
the ancient, the classic "purity of race" which forms the
basis for Nazi action. It is precisely this that the West
Indian tradition abhorred also and tended to break down.
It would have been unlikely that there would have existed
there, in St. Thomas, the incentive to such spurious in-
tegrity of race—such spurious "purity" that it would have
been held laudable for individuals to be governed by its
tenets.*

*The Luchettis were Italian and as they should be, the
Gordons, the Wingwoods, the Monsantos, the Kruegers,
the Hurrards, the Hazels, the Toledos, the Wrights—Casey
Wright! the—it was not only a fact. It was at its best a
revolution of sentiment and of the intelligence. Patti, Gottschalk—whoever it might be came there to understanding
and liberation.*

*Speaking of the modern lie detector used by banks and
the police: They have an appliance which they put on your
arm and it records your reaction to questions. When you
tell a lie your heart goes a little faster and your blood
pressure rises a little. You know how it is when you lie,
you feel it.*

She replied, Well, I don't know.

Didn't you ever lie, we said.

I don't remember; I always got caught.

You remember the chicken you had that broke its leg.
You fixed it with a little splint. And it healed too. When
you went away I had to take care of them. There were a
number of little roosters and all the neighbors complained.
At five o'clock in the morning, Wick aha! They made too
much noise. Mrs. Perham had a big cat and he killed many
of the little ones, but many—and sometimes a big one
too.

(letter to Floss)

*And yet she is the one who says: I am here because I
can't help it, etc., etc. Instead of the obvious and salutary,
Thank you, simply and straightforward without exaggera-
tion or tortuous emphasis—which seldom if ever occurs.
Resistant and relentless to the last—and if caught at it,
profoundly disturbed, depressed, angry.*

I'm here because I can't do anything else (Floss with
tray) Now what do you suppose she means by that? I can't
bother to ask any more, Floss said to me.

Well, it seems that Juliette Farine's mother was very
funny. I don't know whether I told you before. Her husband, M. Barbeau d'Eau de Claire—he was a nobleman,
but she was very *bourgeoise*. He killed himself for honesty.
He grieved that he could not pay and finally he died. But
his wife was the devil.

She was the very devil. She wanted to go back to France
and she didn't have any money. So she painted herself and
made herself look awful, she wanted them to think she was
sick. So they took pity on her and they took her.

But she was very funny. She used to tell my mother.
Once she was sick at night, something she had eaten. But
the *basin*, the big chamber pot, was full. So she had to call
the black man, *un hombre de confianza*, you know a man
in the house. His name was Boucicola. She used to laugh
when she would tell it. He was in his night gown and she
in her night gown with a candle, he with the *basin* on his
head to carry it outside.

If you're going to install yourself I'll go up: *installer*.

Son, is Baldwin going to give up? It says there in the
French paper that he's going to give up.—I don't know,
I have so many things on my mind I don't follow it.—Oh
well, it don't do any harm.

Pop stepped into something that time. It was onerous
for us all, though we didn't know it. It permeated our lives.

Her relation with the Church too was something strange

*—never strong or convincing. Catholic or Protestant both
have always been more than a little suspect with her, the
Catholic because of shallow reliance upon ignorance, upon
"mystery" largely made to order to deceive the unfortunate
and the Protestant because of its direct appeal to reason,
but lack of emotional appeal—and general unintelligence.*

I think I said something that was not true. I must see.
I told him (Bill) that you could not use your eyes as much
as the others to study all night. But that anyhow you were
second in the class.
No. Not second. Sixth.
That's right. I knew I had not said the truth. I must tell
him that.

*Her world has become so small that it is possible now to
sense it whole:* the girls are so different now, they come and
they go and stay at each other's houses all night like that. I
would never stay away from home for even one night. They
always had to come and fetch me.

March 18, 1937
    And so—
                que dieu nous benisse—
                                        Good night

*Certainly her life had a definite form and purpose—not
by any means sentimental: it was based on somewhat rigid
loyalties to the ideal. When she herself was unable to fulfill
her desires for personal accomplishment, she transferred*

her ambitions to her children. That she loved her children goes, perhaps, without saying. But that an uncompromising stubborness toward an ideal preceded that love is nearer to the truth. There was little softness in her, her hands were peculiarly clumsy, short fingered and broad. But not a peasant hand, more bony than muscled. And after arthritis affected them, turning the fingers outward and knobbing the joints, they seemed actually clawish.

That long purpose, outside of herself, made of her a difficult person to live with. It is under these circumstances that weakness, inability in practical management, unwillingness to make up the mind in ordinary affairs becomes so maddening to others. The purpose is cleverly hidden by this means—it lies like an animal in a bush not easily discerned. But when that hidden purpose is thwarted, then the beast is let loose, the donkey, the cat, the snake, the tiger, and the pigeon—anything to gain and maintain an advantage.

That is why Pop said you will see!

That is why there is no love lost between her and any other woman that I ever heard of. It is that ringing of steel against steel, the desire to capture the effective male for her uses—high, to be sure! Therefore, the excuse for domination seems valid. Men! men that accomplish great things are her ideal. She despised women and especially the modern emancipated woman. She would never understand her brazeness, her pretense of being equal with man and militantly asserting that equality. Look at what men can do! she would say. A woman can't do that.

By which she meant: My men can do that and let any

woman try to equal it. But such women are not soft, they drive, they do not comfort—they are too restless, too far gone into the destructive ideal—that is why they are afraid to die: For if their life could have been their end: then they have not lived as they desire.

Son, will you see there in the writing desk if there's a piece of chewing gum there. Right there. I don't do any exercise now so I don't eat so much.

(I found it in place, as usual, two pieces in the green wrapper.)

Do you want the whole piece or the half?

The half will do. Keep the other piece. Put it back where it was.

Funny people! So many ignorant people you cannot conceive. So silly! Like Saint Thomas says, *Pistacle!* (leave it) Something silly that they make a big fuss about.

You made me think of my mother when she got a fresh egg—always put it to her eyes.

Anyway, I am alive and old—and when I came here they told me, Oh! that weather! It will finish you.

When I was young I was crazy for daisies. I thought they were bea-u-ti-ful.

If anything was going on at the other house—I can see Pop! All the lights had to go up. If two cats were coming—

all the lights must go up. That's a little foolish sometimes. It's all right for strangers or a party, but when only a few friends are coming, what's the use?

In Puerto Rico they have a little plant—not a bush, but it lies flat, on the floor. They call it *Muribibi*—dead alive. If you touch it it looks as if it was dead, it collapses. Then after a little while it is alive again. The sensitive plant, yes.

Speaking of Marguerita, an interesting Mexican Indian who has led an extraordinary life in this suburb for over thirty years. She used to work for Mother and has remained steadfastly attached to her to this day: Anyhow I got a good laugh from her today. She says she goes to church every Sunday. Pero no entiendes lo que dice el cure. *I asked her if she understood what the preacher was saying. I knew she didn't.*

"No," she says, "but that's nothing. When they stand up I stand up too. And when they take up a book and open it. Me, too."

"But you can't read it," said Mother.

Marguerita just laughed. "That's nothing. When they turn the page, I turn the page."

About the Author

William Carlos Williams was born in Rutherford, New Jersey, on September 17, 1883. The first years of his school life were spent in the Rutherford public schools. When he had completed the eighth grade, he was taken abroad for a year and a half and attended school in Switzerland and Paris. Returning to America, he attended the Horace Mann High School. A special examination admitted him directly to the medical school of the University of Pennsylvania; he received his M.D. degree in 1906. After a period of internment at the old French Hospital and Child's Hospital in New York City, he became a general practitioner in Rutherford. Except for a short time after the First World War, he has been a doctor in Rutherford ever since.

In 1909, Dr. Williams published a small volume of verse, *Poems*, which was locally printed. Since then he has published some forty books; poetry, short stories, plays, essays and novels. In 1957 his *Selected Letters* appeared. This correspondence covered 52 years and was carried on with many of the literary and artistic pioneers of our time. Dr. Williams has received practically every possible award for his poetry and has been awarded many honorary degrees.